T0339675

TRUE JEW

TRUE JEW

CHALLENGING THE STEREOTYPE

BERNARD BECK

Algora Publishing
New York

Library of Congress Cataloging-in-Publication Data —

Beck, Bernard, 1938-
   True Jew Challenging the Stereotype / Bernard Beck.
      p. cm.
   Includes bibliographical references.
   ISBN 978-0-87586-903-2 (soft cover: alk. paper) — ISBN 978-0-87586-904-9 (hard
cover: alk. paper) — ISBN 978-0-87586-905-6 (ebook) 1. Jews—Identity. 2. Jews—
Political and social conditions. 3. Jews—Cultural assimilation. 4. Judaism—History. I.
Title.
   DS143.B354 2012
   909'.04924—dc23
                              2012001635

Printed in the United States

TABLE OF CONTENTS

Religious suffering is at the same time an expression of real suffering and a protest against real suffering. Religion is the sigh of the oppressed creature, the sentiment of a heartless world, and the soul of a soulless condition. It is the opium of the people.

—Karl Marx

Progress, far from consisting in change, depends on retentiveness. When change is absolute there remains no being to improve and no direction is set for possible improvement: and when experience is not retained, as among savages, infancy is perpetual. Those who cannot remember the past are condemned to repeat it.

—George Santayana

Breathes there the man with soul so dead
Who never to himself hath said,
This is my own, my native land!
Whose heart hath ne'er within him burned,
As home his footsteps he hath turned
From wandering on a foreign strand!
If such there breathe, go, mark him well;
For him no minstrel raptures swell;
High though his titles, proud his name,
Boundless his wealth as wish can claim
Despite those titles, power, and pelf,
The wretch, concentred all in self,
Living, shall forfeit fair renown,
And, doubly dying, shall go down
To the vile dust from whence he sprung,
Unwept, unhonored , and unsung.
    —Sir Walter Scott

Even if you are Catholic, if you live in New York, you're Jewish. If you live in Butte, Montana, you are going to be a goy even if you are Jewish.
    —Lenny Bruce

Introduction — What is a True Jew?

Our grand-daughter Isabel mentioned at dinner one night that she was the only "True Jew" in her class. She lives with her parents in a relatively Jewish suburban community that boasts three synagogues. She explained that by "True Jew" she meant that she was the only Jewish child in her Public School class who has two born-Jewish parents. "Surely, that must be different in Hebrew school," I asked. "Yes," she replied, "A few others in Hebrew School are 'True Jews', but most are not."

This got me to thinking. I asked a number of friends what, in their opinion, is a True Jew. Here, in no particular order, are some of their responses:

> I think the concept of a chosen and special people is central. Another is the historical truth of a beleaguered minority with a shared history of persecution and survival. Both of these have produced the Jewish world view expressed by the leading comedians of the 20th century.

> I think it's a fascinating question, in part because it's no longer religious observance that unites us as Jews yet we all "feel" very Jewish. Maybe the concept is actually contained in the word itself. We are Jew-ish, not quite a True Jew but a Jew-lite, I think you and I and Judy all think of ourselves as "good Jews" but my Hassidim think I am a gentile. When I talk to them, I think that just studying the Torah, the Mishnah etc all day does not make for a good person or a True Jew.

In any event, thinking about your question, I think it's the idea of Jewish exceptionalism and the Jew-as-outsider that has created this bond of peoplehood and of a True Jew — not going to Shul or davening every morning.

—Julie

Let me think about this for a while.
How long do I have?
A true Jew is hard to describe.
The fact that it's a rhyme makes its posed question all the more difficult.
And "true."
What's that?
I once asked my painting teacher what true green looked like and he said I was just trying to annoy him rather than shmear the colors on as I was supposed to be doing, and questions about true or not true were irrelevant.
So true Jew.
Am I a true Jew or a false Jew or a derivative type modeling myself on Rivka or Sarah or some other Jewess rather than find out the true Jew I could be if I were true to myself,
whatever "self" actually means.
So I'll get back to you because your question is sending me in circles looking for the true me to answer true-ly what I think...now that you pose the question.
Very Truly Jewly yours,
—Judi

Anyone who believes that they are a Jew is a 'true Jew.' If you are born to a Jewish mother you are a true Jew. If you convert to Judaism and you believe in your heart you are a Jew you are a 'true Jew'. If you don't care a bit about religion or politics — whoever you are if you say you are a TRUE JEW you are a true Jew...

—VS

From a genetic point of view, a true Jew is one whose mother is Jewish. To me that is the easiest and most concrete way to identify a "true Jew". After that it becomes murky, because being Jewish involves more that the observance of the tenets of Judaism. So much of our identity is wrapped up in our culture and our culture is so diverse, whether Sephardic or Ashkenazi. Those of us who identify ourselves as Jews each have our own particular reason for doing so. The Hasidim wouldn't consider either of us Jewish, yet I see them as a sect of Judaism, not as "true Jews". Everything seems to be degrees — among the Orthodox: The right doesn't consider the more modern moderate Jews as true Jews, so forget about everyone within the Conservative and Reform movements; and everything dilutes from there. Yet, if you were to ask anyone within any of these divisions if they were Jewish the answer would be unequivocally — yes. Also, there are many Jews who don't have any religious affiliation, and see themselves as more cultural Jews — identifying with certain foods one considers "Jewish", sharing a certain kind of humor — and those who consider themselves Jewish from a Zionist point of view. So, I guess, like beauty, the labeling of who is a true Jew, is in the eye of the beholder.

—Barbara

Those of us whose convictions parallel Humanistic Judaism, pretty much, define real or true Jews as follows. They

1) identify as or call themselves "Jews",

2) belong to the ethno-historic entity called "The Jewish People" (Klal Yisrael),

3) congregate (or attempt to) in Jewish communities to affirm their beliefs to celebrate their Jewishness and humanity,

4) study and interpret Jewish history, philosophy and traditions, and

5) endeavor to perpetuate Jewishness to future generations.

The underlying philosophy pretty much follows the writings of Baruch Spinoza, Martin Buber, Albert Einstein, etc.

—Marvin

I think the Hebrew prophet Micah said it all when he said "O man, what is good; And what does the LORD require of you But to do justice, to love kindness, And to walk humbly with your G-d?".

—Ted

A True Jew is a very interesting term, as Truth is a question of a subjective opinion.

To me, anyone who was born into the Jewish faith, or has at least one Jewish parent has a membership in the club of the Jewish People. But as in any other club, there are rules and guidelines to follow. If you do not "obey" you can be denied this membership.

Mentioning this metaphor means that anyone who is genetically Jewish does not get an automatic membership unless they follow practical prescribed ways. A Jewish person who is unethical and unjust, who does not care about humanity and is selfish cannot be, in my mind, a True Jew, but can still be Jewish.

—Ziona

The question makes me uneasy. Saying there is a "True Jew" implies that there is a category "*Not* True Jews" — that one Jew can be "better" or "truer" — it implies a hierarchy. For me, there can be differences in the way we practice or observe Judaism.

I'm reminded of a friend who said: You want to know what a good Jew is? I'll tell you what a good Jew is. Anyone who does less than me is a bad Jew. And, anyone who does more than me is a fanatic.

—Judy

Human nature is human nature. But ultimately, it is the nature of nurture and other experiences that bring to light and life one's personality. The development of personality, Jewish or otherwise, does not occur in a vacuum. The opinions, philosophies, values, beliefs, perspectives and personalities, of parents, relatives and friends regarding politics, race, religion, socio-economic status, anti-semitism, Israel, the arts and education are all contributing factors. The influence of teachers, travel, theater and what one reads help shape personality. The degree to which a Jew has been marginalized or experienced anti-semitism may influence personality. But do these factors result in a definitive Jewish personality? Is there a Jewish essence?

It is easy for some to succumb to and even perpetuate stereotypes regarding the character, behavior or manner of expression of Jews. Are all Jews Shylocks, Tevyas or a little of each? Some say Jews all have the same values, beliefs, personality and perceptions. But do all Jews see the glass half empty or half full? Even some Jews may claim that there is a "special little something" about the Jewish personality. But do the characters and personalities portrayed in Jewish jokes capture the essence? Are the characteristics and personalities of Jews so different than other cultures? And finally, an increased awareness of other cultures and the effect of cultural homogeneity due to globalization suggests that personality differences are flat. Given the diverse nature of nurture, and the vast array of experiences that have the potential to shape personality, there is no such thing as a definitive Jewish personality.

—Steve

The personality of a "True Jew" evolved over time and through opportunities and rejections. Today's "True Jew" has lost the sharpness of definition that his parents had. But still, I would say that the characteristics of a True Jew are Humor, Determination, Aggressiveness, and an emphasis on education to enhance achievement. Today's True Jew is Generous without being Altruistic. Above all, the main characteristic of a True Jew is humor.

—Sandy

Growing up in Israel, I was trained to think of Jews as a culture that is rounded with sets of emotional and intellectual embodiment of Jewish history, understanding of religious practices, and commitment to Israel as the center of Jewish life and tradition that makes our nation. Growing up in a Zionist family who immigrated to then Palestine early in the 1900s, the definition of a Jew was and is one who lives anywhere but is free to define himself as a Jew without fear of discrimination. Living in Israel was a personal choice to finding intellectual, emotional, religious and economic freedom from oppressors, not necessarily related to religious practice. I never considered that being and feeling Jewish is defined by an affiliation with a religious organization. On the contrary, early in childhood I learned to view religion-practicing Jews in Israel with antagonism and disgrace due to their refusal to serve in the military with the rationale that they are doing their part through prayers.

Upon arriving in the USA, I realized that Jews in this country define themselves in terms of affiliation with synagogue, even if they attended once a year. In addition, for many Jews their identity stems from being Bar or Bat Mitzvah, a practice that I learned to view in Israel as a necessary social obligation (rite of passage) of coming of age and definitely not as a religious definition or identity. My disappointment was that most had a limited understanding of history, ethics, religious practices or meaning. Yet, they are part of the Jewish nation and clearly define themselves as "True Jew".

Growing up Zionist to the bones, defining myself according to religious guidelines was a strange notion that I still regard as limited and one which undermines that rich Jewish heritage. Despite religious contention that they and only they preserved the survival of the Jewish nation throughout time, it is historically erroneous and factually unsupported. Using your earlier writing as a framework, that argument is a great marketing success (the big lie). The evidence is that Jews who cherished their cultural heritage and identity were the safeguards of Jewish existence that enabled the continual survival of our small nation and Jews around the world. Our fellow Jews, who are sitting in Yeshiva or Chaderim, in my view, lack the richness of Jewish history, tradition and national identity and therefore are not representative of what is a "True Jew".

What makes a "True Jew" in my mind is anyone who wants to be part of the culture and is able to integrate successfully by embodying the various aspects of Judaism. For example, a "True Jew" in my mind is a person who understands and appreciates our history, our distinct interpersonal connections, music, religion, language and strong identity with Israel and Jews around the world. We often recognize a Jew wherever he or she is without the distinct clothing or institutional affiliation. Our uniqueness is expressed in style, behavior, and expression.

One appalling behavior by the religious bodies in Israel these days is to limit the definition of Jews to those born to Jewish mothers who are white, who came to Israel from Russia, Poland other European countries and USA. In my mind, anyone that defines herself or himself as Jewish, regardless of skin color and origin, is entitled to belong to our nation. As Jews are free to migrate to other religious organizations, so too non-Jews should be allowed to become "True Jews". Jews today (50%) intermarry and have children from these unions who often define themselves as being Jewish even though their mothers are not Jewish. To disqualify or marginalize them as Jews is unethical and irrational in our time, no matter how logical an argument it was in the past. Furthermore, Israel's law of the Right to Return insists that Jews of all colors and national origin who define themselves as Jewish and can demonstrate historical, ethnic and cultural tradition should be considered "True Jews".

—Dan

In the open society of America, I am assimilated but clearly identify myself as Jewish, though not observant. I say Jewish instead of a Jew because it's a cultural identity. It occurs to me that a sense of being Jewish has burned into my core during my life's experiences. It's not so much what makes me Jewish, but being Jewish, how does that express itself in my life. It's so blended into my being and daily life that I don't think about it until someone like you asks. When thinking about it, I see willingly being an outsider, questioning authority and everything else—not to be oppositional but for personal and more informed understanding, being passionate about learning, feeling satisfaction when Jews gain and being hurt by their losses, being a good friend, respecting and looking to be of help to others even in modest ways, and wanting to do something useful in society. It's hard to distinguish which features are Jewish and which are just my nature, or maybe these are blended.

—Irving

Asking what is a "true Jew" as opposed to a "plain" Jew brings up personal biases and values. You will probably get as many opinions as the number of people you ask. To my mind, a "plain" Jew is basically a member of the tribe. They identify with the Jewish people and share Jewish values and culture. A "true Jew" goes further. They belong to a synagogue which they attend more than twice a year. They support Jewish charities, are concerned with events in Israel, and will speak up for Jews and Israel whenever attacked.

—Conrad

A True Jew is anyone who defines themselves as such.

—Judy

As we see, things are seldom what they seem. The owner of the largest car or the biggest house may not be the wealthiest in the community; the venerable doctor might not be the most knowledgeable; the most crowded restaurant might not be the best. It's a matter of perception. These "impressions" are a kind of shorthand that our mind uses to assist in the decision-making process. But, although they are convenient, they are often wrong.

Appearance is everything. We teach our children: "If you want to be successful, you have to look successful," and "First impressions last." We evaluate politicians by their handshake and the way they speak; we evaluate entertainers by a whole host of criteria that are not related to their performing skills; and we evaluate religious leaders by their degree of "spirituality" which can include dress, voice, vocabulary, and gender.

One of the most common stereotypes is "authenticity." We have an image in our minds of what a specific "authentic" person would look like. A laborer should look like a laborer, an executive should look like an executive, a computer nerd, a stock exchange trader, a gardener, a priest, a librarian[1], an author; we have very clear images in our minds of what they should look like.

The traditional stereotypical image of a "True Jew" is, unfortunately and inaccurately, often the "Fiddler on the Roof"[2] shtetle image; or its ultra orthodox haredi equivalent[3] today. This book is a historic exploration of the accuracy of that stereotype.

* * *

At the start of the Common Era, Jews lived throughout the Roman Empire and Byzantium. They had been primarily farmers but now they were becoming merchants as well. Israel was on the trade route and the Jews of Israel realized that they could achieve greater success in commerce than in farming.

Many Jews emigrated to nearby lands and established Jewish outposts there. The countries of Algeria, Ethiopia, Libya, Morocco, Syria, Yemen, and Tunisia provided hospitable and fertile ground for the establishment of Jewish businesses. Jews seeking commercial opportunities ventured as far as China and Azerbaijan in the east and Spain in the west.

Judaism as a religion was flourishing; and conversions to Judaism were frequent and common. Jewish adventurers and mercenaries were prominent members of the Roman armies. Anti-Semitism did not exist in the Roman Empire.

There were at least four and a half million Jews in the world.[4]

---

1 Consider the movie stereotype of the librarian who "lets down her hair."
2 Sholom Aleichem, the author of the "Tevye" stories on which "Fiddler" was based, was the son of a wealthy merchant who, as a result of business losses, moved to the small town where the Tevye stories are located. Aleichem received a traditional Jewish education but also attended a state school. He was employed by a Jewish landowner as a tutor but was forced to leave after the discovery of his secret romance with the young lady he tutored. At the age of 24, he married his former pupil and eventually returned to her father's estate to function as executor.
3 Black hat, beard, and long frock coat for men; wig, hat, and frumpy dress for women.
4 Some contemporary estimates place this number as high as six million.

Over the next five hundred years, as the Pharisees and their successors the rabbis imposed increasingly strict religious and secular rules, the official Jewish population dropped from four and a half million to under one and a half million.

After the destruction of the Temple in 70 C.E., the *rabbis* became not only the arbiters of the religious norm for the Jews, but also the recorders and reporters of Jewish history. From that time on, what we know of Jewish history and culture was reported through their eyes.

But, as we will see in the coming chapters, Jewish history was not always the way the rabbis reported. More than half of the world's Jews dropped out of active participation in rabbinic society. But, although these Jews dropped out of *rabbinic* Judaism, they didn't completely leave the fold. And in the eighteenth and nineteenth and twentieth centuries, when new religious options presented themselves, and traditional rabbinic Judaism was at its weakest, these Jews returned in fantastic numbers.

Chapter 1. The Enigma and the Solution

The Start of the Diaspora

The Second Temple was destroyed in 70 C.E. It had stood in Jerusalem since 516 BCE It, in turn, had replaced Solomon's Temple which was built in the 10th century BCE and was destroyed in 586 BCE Thus, with the exception of the seventy years between the two temples, Israel had never been without its most sacred shrine, the "Bais Hamikdash", which had been the center of Jewish sacrificial worship.

In the two hundred years preceding the destruction of the Second Temple, Israel had been in a state of constant chaos. In 167 BCE the Seleucids[5] attempted to impose Hellenism on the Jewish population. This brought about the successful Maccabean Revolt in CE 164 which was led by the priest Mattathias,[6] a member of the Hasmonean family.

In 63 BCE after a hundred years of chaotic conflict-ridden Hasmonean rule, Israel was re-conquered by the Romans. Twenty years later the Parthians (from what is now northeastern Iran) invaded Judea and

---

5 The Seleucid Empire was created out of the eastern conquests of Alexander the Great and was a major center of Hellenistic culture.

6 After the Seleucid persecutions began, Mattathias, when commanded by a Seleucid to offer a sacrifice to the Greek gods, not only refused to do so but slew another Jew who had stepped forward to do so. He then attacked the government official who had required the act.

---

seized Jerusalem. Three years later, Herod the Great, who had been designated "King of the Jews" by the Roman Senate, took back Judea. He has been described as "a madman who murdered his own family[7]", but he is also known for his colossal building projects in Jerusalem and elsewhere, including the rebuilding of the Second Temple in Jerusalem (sometimes referred to as Herod's Temple). Herod ruled for thirty-seven oppressive and chaotic years, thirty-four of them after capturing Jerusalem.

This unstable environment provided a fertile ground for the growth of Jewish religious sects with varying approaches to religious observance.

Flavius Josephus, the foremost contemporary historian of this period, described five major sects. He called three of them, the Sadducees, Essenes, and Pharisees, religious. The remaining two, the Zealots and Sicarii, he described as criminal because they were extreme nationalists whose religious beliefs were incorporated with their political convictions.

The Sadducees believed in strict adherence to the written Torah, and they believed that the Torah was the only legitimate source of Jewish law. They declared that there is no such thing as fate, and that "we are ourselves the causes of what is good, and receive what is evil from our own folly."

The Essenes[8] rejected all forms of pleasure as evil. They believed that the "conquest" of our passions is a virtue and "they guard[ed] against the lascivious behavior of women, and are persuaded that none of them [women] preserve their fidelity to one man."

The Pharisees believed in an oral law along with the Torah. They were also, depending on the time, a political party, a social movement, and a school of thought. They believed that a higher spirit (God) has control of our lives, and they preached that many, but not all human actions, are ordained by God. After the destruction of the Second Temple, the Pharisaic sect was reconfigured as rabbinic Judaism, which ultimately became the basis for all modern-day forms of Judaism.

Josephus considered the Sicariis and the Zealots to be terrorists. The Sicariis' most notable tactic was the use of short daggers (called sicaris) to kill people. Although they were not terrorists in the modern sense,

---

7   Herod is reputed to have had nine wives and at least fourteen children.
8   Jesus is believed to have been an Essene, and vestiges of Essene philosophy can be seen in Christianity.

this method of murdering people in crowded places before slipping away was designed to cause extreme anxiety among the surrounding populace, and thus terrorize them. They primarily focusedprimarilyfocused their attacks on Jewish notables and elites associated with the priesthood with whom they disagreed. The Zealots, on the other hand, aimed their violence against Romans.

Some of the lesser groups that appeared during the tumultuous years following the destruction of the Temple were the Jewish Christians who attempted to blend the new messianic Christian beliefs with the traditional practices of Judaism; the Hellenistic Jews who sought to establish a Jewish religious tradition within the culture and language of Hellenism; and the Samaritans who considered personal sacrifice an important part of their religion and did not accept the Mishna and the Talmud. Some of the rabbis and scholars in the second century still considered these fringe groups as belonging to the Jewish fold and held out hope of their eventual inclusion in Judaism. But Rabbi Judah ha-Nassi[9], the most influential rabbi of the time, rejected them and equated them to Gentiles.

The apparent disparity among these Jewish sects was not very different from today's various permutations of Jewish religious observance which run the gamut from the ultra orthodox Haredi movement[10] to the Secular Humanists, each asserting its authenticity and claiming its rightful place in the spectrum of Jewish belief.

Judaism lost its moorings after the destruction of the Temple. While the Temple was in existence, there had been priests and there had been the Temple ceremonies. Every year at the appointed times the priests performed various religious rites. There had been sacrifices, and pilgrimages, and wonderful ritual, and huge ceremonies which were attended by all Jews who were able[11]. Here is a partial description[12] of the Yom Kippur ceremony in the Temple as translated by Rev. Dr. A. TH. Philips, in the

---

9   The redactor of the Mishna, and therefore an interested party.

10   A Haredi representative in Israel was recently given bodyguard protection after threats against his life came from other Haredis.

11   Those Jews who, for various reasons, were not able to make the pilgrimage to Jerusalem, made financial contributions.

12   From the personal tone of this description, it sounds like an eye witness.

Prayer Book for the Day of Atonement (Hebrew Publishing Company, New York, p. 248-9):

> As soon as the watchman proclaimed that the morning star had risen, they spread a veil of fine linen to conceal him from the sight of the people; he (the high priest) then put off his linen garments, bathed and put on the golden garments; he then washed his hands and feet, and slew the daily burnt-offering of the morning, and commanded another (priest) to complete it; he received the blood and sprinkled it; he then went to offer incense, and trim the lamps; he then offered the burnt offering, and poured out the drink offering, performing the service of the burnt offering according to order; he then entered the chamber, parvo which was in the holy temple, where they again spread a veil before him as at first; there he washed his hands and feet, and put off his golden garments; he then went and bathed, put on the white garments, and washed his hands and feet. These were costly garments from Egypt, of the value of eighteen minim; they were most beautiful, and fit to be worn by him who ministered to the King of Glory! He then drew near to his own bull, which was placed between the porch and the altar, with his face towards the west, and his head turned towards the south; he sustained his hand on his head, and made confession of his transgressions, not concealing any.

> And thus did he say: "O God! I now acknowledge that I have sinned; I have committed iniquity; I have transgressed against thee; even I, and my household. I beseech thee now by thy ineffable name, to forgive, pardon, and grant expiation, for the sins, iniquities, and transgressions which I have committed against thee; even I, and my household; as it is written in the law of thy servant Moses, from thy glorious mouth, 'for on this day, shall he (the high priest) make atonement for you, to cleanse you from all your sins before the Lord.'"

> And the priests and the people who stood in the court, when they heard the glorious, tremendous, and ineffable name, proceed from the mouth of the high priest, with sanctity and purity, they kneeled and prostrated themselves, falling on their faces, and saying, "blessed be the name of his glorious majesty, for ever and ever."

> He (the high priest) also was attentive, to finish pronouncing the ineffable name at the same time, when they who blessed the name of the lord finished, and to whom he said, "Ye shall be clean." And thou, in thy great goodness didst awaken thy mercy and grantest forgiveness to thy pious servant.

It is clear from this description that very little was required of the Jews in the way of participation — other than to be observers and to be, by their presence, part of the ritual. In addition to Yom Kippur there were many other holidays including the three major pilgrimage holidays: Succot, Pesach, and Shavuot, each with its own unique ritual.

After the destruction of the Temple, the Jews had initially separated into many denominations. But only two, the Pharisees and the Sadducees had substantial following, and in the end, only the Pharisees[13] remained.

The Jewish Transformation

In the first one hundred and fifty years of the Common Era the Jews fought three wars of independence against the Romans. Nearly a million Jews died or were enslaved as a result of those three wars. But for the next three hundred years Jews lived in reasonable peace and security in the Roman Empire. If the Jewish population growth rate had kept pace with the general population growth rate there would have been approximately 5.5 million[14] Jews in the world by the year 500. But instead, the Jewish population had dropped to 1.4 million. Apparently, well over three million Jews had *disappeared*. This precipitous and unexplained drop was followed by a further slow decline that lasted for more than a thousand years.

What happened to them? Where did they go?

I have presented this question to various scholars and essentially received a shrug of the shoulders. Some say vaguely "pogroms". But when I confront them with the numbers, they smile benevolently and change the subject. Others say, vaguely, "conversions," but when I ask them to be more specific, they too smile benevolently and change the subject. The truth of this matter is that there is no apparent answer. If we say that the Jews converted to Christianity, that would mean that in those five hundred years, nearly three Jews converted for each Jew who remained in the faith. This is not accurate historically nor is it possible logically. As to the theory that Jews were slaughtered by the Romans, this too is not historically accurate. The Romans were generally tolerant of other religions, and there are no records either in Jewish history or in world history that support this theory.

---

13   and a few Samaritans
14   Allowing for the loss of 1 million Jews plus their potential children.

The key events that affected Jews during those first centuries were the three disastrous Jewish rebellions against Rome in 67, 115 and 135 C.E. Each of these revolutions resulted in horrible loss of Jewish lives. An estimated 100,000 Jews were killed or sold into slavery as a result of the first "Great" revolution; the Second Jewish–Roman War led to the death of more than 200,000 Jews; and the third revolution, the so called Bar Kochba revolution, which was the bloodiest of all, resulted in the death and enslavement of 580,000 Jews, both combatant and civilian. The devastation as a result of these three brutal wars was horrifying. The total deaths and enslavements, both combatant and civilian, are generally estimated to be nearly one million Jews. This was a terrible loss.

The first Jewish–Roman War began in the year 66 C.E. as a result of anti-taxation protests and attacks upon Roman citizens. There was also, at the same time, an undercurrent of internal Jewish religious tensions. The Jews had become embroiled in a civil conflict which split the resistance among two terrorist factions; the Sicarii led by Simon Bar Giora, and the Zealots led by John of Gischala. This internal fighting seriously weakened the Jewish forces[15]. The war ended when the Roman Legions under Titus besieged and destroyed the centre of rebel resistance in Jerusalem, and defeated the remaining Jewish strongholds. The siege of Jerusalem, the capital city, which had begun early in the war, ended in the summer of 70 when the Romans breached the walls of Jerusalem, ransacked and burned nearly the entire city and destroyed the Second Temple.

The failure of the revolution and the destruction of Jerusalem and the Temple left a spiritual vacuum in the Jewish world. Many of the Jewish rebels were scattered or sold into slavery.

Half a century later, the third and last major rebellion of the Jewish–Roman Wars, known as the Bar Kokhba revolt (132–136 C.E.), resulted in the exile of the remaining Jews. The outbreak initially took the Romans by surprise and the struggle lasted for three years before the revolt was brutally crushed in the summer of 135. In what may have been one of the most catastrophic pronouncements in Jewish history, the Jewish sage

---

15 Some historians report that one of the Jewish warring factions actually invited the Romans in to Jerusalem in order to defeat their opponents.

Rabbi Akiva had proclaimed that Simon bar Kokhba, the commander of the revolt, was the Messiah. Akiva hoped that this heroic figure could restore Israel and he indulged the possibility that he was acting in accord with the biblical "star" prophecy: "There shall come a star out of Jacob".[16]

This messianic claim in favor of Bar Kokhba sharply deepened the schism between the Jews and the Christians who believed that the true Messiah was Jesus. Modern historians have come to view the Bar-Kokhba Revolt as being of decisive historic importance both for the continuity of the Jewish people and the schism between Christians and Jews. The massive destruction and loss of life that was the result of this third revolution marked the true beginning of the Jewish Diaspora. They note that, unlike the aftermath of the first two Jewish–Roman Wars, Jewish political authority was suppressed far more brutally. As a result of the exile from Jerusalem, Jewish religious leadership divided into two distinct groups. One group moved from Jerusalem to the Babylonian Jewish community; the other moved west from Jerusalem to the Israeli city of Yavne. In the absence of the Temple, the spiritual guidance for the now scattered Jews was provided by these two Pharisee intellectual centers.

The New Jews

Surprisingly, in spite of all of the wars, forced exile, and destruction, it was not difficult to be a Jew during the first centuries of the Common Era, and many Jews fared relatively well. Judaism, as a religion was fully tolerated within the Roman Empire. Jews were both farmers and merchants; some were even "gentleman farmers" who split their time between the farm and the city. Some Jews were missionaries who successfully proselytized among the pagan Romans, some Jews were mercenaries, and some Jews were merchants who traveled freely within the Roman Empire.

In nearly every part of the Jewish Diaspora in the years immediately following the destruction of the Second Temple, the Jews lived clustered together in the cities. They doubtless possessed farms and orchards in the suburbs; but agriculture was no longer, as it had been in Judea, their almost exclusive occupation. In Alexandria, they were engaged in com-

---

16 "Bar Kokhba" means "son of a star" in the Aramaic language

merce and navigation, and especially in the mechanical trades. At their gatherings in the synagogue they were grouped by their respective handicrafts. The Jews of Italy and Greece, for example, were weavers, tentmakers, butchers, tavern-keepers, singers, comedians, painters, jewelers, physicians, and even poets and men of letters, in addition to the preachers, lawyers, and theologians. At the end of the fourth century, the highest class of citizens of some cities of southern Italy seems to have been composed entirely, or at least principally, of Jews; a proof of their prosperity. In Egypt under the Ptolemies, Jews were soldiers, civil functionaries, and generals. It is noteworthy that rarely before the Middle Ages are the Jews referred to as money-lenders, bankers, or usurers. These callings seem to have been forced upon them much later by circumstances and as a result of special legislation.

Theoretically, because of the Jewish "laws of purity", there was little socializing between the Jews and the pagans. These rules were not, however, always and everywhere observed with the same rigor. Evidence of this appears in the Judeo-Alexandrian literature with its strong Hellenic infusion; in some of the professions pursued by the Jews; and in the general and almost exclusive employment of Greeks by the Jews of the Diaspora, even for religious services. In Rome, many Jewish tombstones bear inscriptions that are first in Greek and then in Latin. Their Hebrew words are limited to a few hallowed formulas, and almost all the proper names are in Greek or Latin.

Above all it was the Jewish activity of religious proselytism that brought about the intimate contact and the reciprocal penetration of the two civilizations. The act of proselytism was one of the most distinctive traits of Judaism during the Greco–Roman epoch. This zeal to make converts, which taken by today's values seems to be incompatible with Jewish mores, is attested to by numerous Roman and Jewish documents.

In agreement with the customs of the time, various methods were used to expand the Jewish population.

The most brutal proselytism was forced circumcision as had been imposed by John Hyrcanus on the Idumeans. Next was the conversion of slaves owned by Jews as their individual property.

The most successful proselytism by far, was the moral propaganda, by word, example, and book. The practical and legal character of Judaism's doctrine, which furnished a rule of life for every occasion, appealed strongly to the fragmented Roman society. The purity and simplicity of Jewish theology and the mystery and appeal of its customs — especially the welcome Sabbath rest, captivated the high-minded. In addition, Jewish literature recalled the poets, thinkers, sibyls and the greatest geniuses of ancient Greece. In brief, Judaism was a religion that was supple and elastic while appearing rigid. It was a religion which knew how to be at once authoritative and liberal, idealistic and materialistic, a philosophy for the strong, a superstition for the weak, and a hope of salvation for all.

Judaism did not demand of its proselytes, at the outset, full and complete adoption of Jewish law. The neophyte was at first simply a "friend" to the Jewish customs, observing the least demanding ones like the Friday night candle-lighting ritual, the Sabbath, and the abstention from pork. His sons frequented the synagogues and learned Jewish law. By degrees, habit accomplished the rest. At last the proselyte took the decisive step: he received the rite of circumcision, and took the bath of purity (mikvah). Occasionally, in order to accentuate his conversion, the convert even adopted a Hebraic name. By the third generation, according to Deuteronomy, there should exist no distinction between the Jew by race and the Jew by adoption.

This gradual entrance into the fold of Judaism must have been a frequent occurrence in the first and second centuries. Efforts have been made to distinguish between the Jews by birth and the proselytes, the "gerim" of the Hebrew texts, but it would seem more accurate to consider these terms as synonymous, while admitting various degrees in proselytism. Those proselytes who were in the early stages of conversion were naturally more numerous than those who had been circumcised. The number of female proselytes substantially exceeded that of the males, a circumstance which may be accounted for by the fear of circumcision.

Judaism in this way made numerous converts during the first two or three centuries. Jewish proselytes were found in large numbers in every country of the Diaspora. Some pagan authors, struck by this phenomenon, even attempted to distinguish the Jews by race from the Jews by adoption. In Antioch a large portion of the Greek population Judaized in the time of Josephus; and although they became Christians in the days of John Chrysostom[17], they had not forgotten the way to the synagogues.

The enormous growth of Judaism in Egypt, Cyprus, and Cyrene (modern day Libya) cannot be accounted for without supposing an abundant infusion of Gentiles. Jewish proselytism was equally effective in the upper and lower classes of society, and Jewish propaganda did not meet with any resistance in the east other than the attachment of the populations to their national religions. No Greek law can be found that was designed to repress Jewish proselytism.

The Roman government, however, showed less indulgence, especially after the three Jewish revolutions which revealed the hatred of the Jews toward their conquerors. While The Romans respected the religious liberty and the national customs of the Jews, severe measures were taken to prevent them from securing recruits, whom the Romans, in their patriotism, looked upon as deserters. After the third revolution Jews were forbidden to circumcise anyone other than their own sons. The circumcision of a non-Jew, even if a slave, was punished with death and confiscation. Both the Roman citizen who submitted himself or who submitted his slave to this operation, and the surgeon who performed the operation, were punished.

The preceding description of Jewish life in the first centuries of the Common Era is based on information from the Jewish Encyclopedia which concludes with this very telling entry:

> The effect of these [anti circumcision] laws was far-reaching, but in a direction different from that purposed by their authors. It is true the increase of the Jewish sect was checked; all the more so since in Talmudic circles the tendencies hostile to proselytism gained decidedly the upper hand. The enfeebling of Judaism, however, did not work to the profit of the pagan religions, which no longer had any hold upon the population. The half-proselytes, having no chance of becoming complete Jews, lent a readier ear to the evangelical preaching; and *it was among these that Christianity made its first and its most numerous conquests.* (italics mine)

---

17 John Chrysostom is known in Christianity chiefly as a preacher, theologian and liturgist, particularly in the Eastern Orthodox Church. Among his sermons, eight directed against Judaizing Christians remain controversial for their impact on the development of Christian antisemitism.

Charles Raddock, writing in *Portrait of a People* (Judaica Press, New York 1967, Book 1, p. 143) about the Jews in the third century describes a Diaspora not unlike today:

There were six to seven million[18] Jews, it has been estimated, throughout the [Roman] empire without any base now of national cohesion. If they had reason to wonder whether their sacred shrine (The Temple) had not been a mere tool in the hands of clerical opportunists who always wooed foreign interventionists or supported great landowners, they had none the less taken pride in that capitol edifice. Regardless of political dissention which may have forced them out of the country, or economic opportunity opening in an expanding colonial empire, which had tempted them to emigrate from Judea, they [had] always contributed to its upkeep, even as their ancestors did in the days of King Solomon

Though they now had synagogues everywhere, [they] would not forget for some time the pilgrim holidays in Jerusalem, the festivals, music, camaraderie and gaiety of the ancient city. From Babylon they used to come, on annual cruises, and from Damascus and Asia Minor, Alexandria and Elephantine, Cyrenaica, Macedonia, and North Africa, even from Rome itself. If they could not manage to take the cruise, they would double their contributions that year to the Temple.[19]

So it seems that even in the early years of Christianity, Jewish population numbers were trending higher. Jews were proselytizing with such great success that the Romans sought ways to slow them down. After all, the Jews were offering a very attractive alternative to the Roman pagan worship. The Jewish population was actually increasing. And then, Christianity began to take hold.

The first Christian services followed essentially a "Christianized" synagogue liturgical framework, and met in parishioner's homes. They continued many of the patterns of Judaism; adapting the synagogue's liturgy, prayer, and readings of sacred scripture to Christian use. Sacred events in the Jewish religious calendar and Jewish practices such as fasting and charity were initially retained as well.

But within a relatively short time Christians and Jews clarified their respective religious practices in such a way as to make them mutually exclusive. The Judeo-Christians in the Christian community, who continued to insist that the laws on circumcision applied to Christians, were demonized by their opponents. This differentiation in the laws of cir-

---

18 I have used the more conservative 4.5 million figure.
19 The powerful Psalm 137 (If I forget thee O Jerusalem) expresses this emotion.

cumcision made Christianity an attractive alternative to Judaism for prospective proselytes. It clearly defied Jewish religious tenets and thus was a major breaking point between Christianity and Judaism. Around 85 CE, in a further widening of the chasm between Christians and Jews, Rabbi Yohanan ben Zakkai, the great sage of Yavne, is said to have condemned all who claimed the Messiah had already come.

Early Church historian Eusebius of Caesarea records that in the first century the ethnically Jewish leadership of the church was replaced by committed Christian leadership. Though Jesus had proclaimed that he had no intention of abrogating the Torah, but of fulfilling it, early Christianity no longer considered itself part of Judaism. Because of this very definite schism the percentage of Jews who converted to any form of Christianity was extremely small.

Initially, the early Christians suffered sporadic persecution in Rome, but by the 4th century, the emperor Constantine made Christianity the favored religion of the Roman Empire.

In contrast to the ascendancy of Christianity, Judaism suffered a number of severe setbacks. Until the late first century, Judaism was a legal religion with the protection of Roman law. Observant Jews had special rights, including the privilege of abstaining from civic pagan rites. But from the start of the second century C.E. onwards the situation of the Jews became more precarious.

Heinrich Graetz, in his monumental nineteenth century *History of the Jews*[20], picks up the narrative:

> After the death of Jesus, a small group of a hundred and twenty persons formed a Christian community through the energy of Paul. He endeavored to win over the Roman pagans by the belief in the resurrection of Christ, and the Jews by the belief that the appearance of the Messiah had proved the validity of the Jewish Law. Christianity began a new element in religious history, but the doctrine that Paul taught; that traditional Jewish Law was unnecessary, had sown the seed of dissension. The followers of Jesus were divided into two great parties, which were arrayed in sharp opposition. On the one hand, were the Judeo-Christians, and, on the other, the Heathen-Christians. The Judeo-Christians were closely connected with Judaism; they observed the Jewish laws in all their details,

---

20 I have adapted this material from Graetz's *History of the Jews* which is in 5 volumes and was published in 1895 by The Jewish Publication Society, Philadelphia, PA.

and pointed to the example of Jesus, who himself had lived according to Jewish laws. Even the great devotion of the Judeo-Christians to Jesus did not separate them from Judaism. They considered him as a holy and morally great man who was descended in the natural way from the race of David; the son of David who had advanced the kingdom of heaven because he taught men to live modestly and in poverty, like the Essenes, from whose midst, in fact, Christianity had sprung.

In opposition to these were the Heathen-Christians. They seized on the term "Son of God," which had been used to mean "holy man" and they interpreted it according to their own mode of thought, as meaning God's actual Son, a conception which was as clear and acceptable to the Heathen-Christians as it was strange and repulsive to the Judeo-Christians.

Once the idea of a Son of God was accepted, it became necessary to eliminate from the life of Jesus all those traits which appertained to him as a human being, such as his natural birth from parents. The statement developed that this Son of God was born of a virgin through the Holy Ghost. Thus, the first great difference between the Judeo-Christians and the Heathen-Christians lay in their views concerning the person of Jesus. The Judeo-Christians honored him as the son of David, and the Heathen-Christians worshiped him as the Son of God.

The second point turned on the emphasis that was put on the traditional laws of Judaism. The Heathen-Christians paid but little attention to the laws relating to the community of property and contempt for riches, which were the chief ends of the Essenes. There arose strained relations and a mutual dislike between the Judeo-Christian and the Heathen-Christian congregations, which became more bitter with time. Paul and his disciples were fiercely hated by the Jewish Christians. And they continued, even after his death, to use expressions of contempt against "the circumcised apostle who only spread error". The leaders of the Heathen-Christians did not hesitate to reply in a similar strain. In the larger Christian congregations the two sects often fell into distinct groups and became isolated from each other. In the circular letters, which the chiefs of the various Christian parties were accustomed to send to the communities, they made use of sharp or condemnatory observations against the opponents of the opinions which they held to be the only true ones. Even the stories of the birth of Jesus, his works, sufferings, death and resurrection, were colored by the views of the two parties, who put teachings and sayings into the mouth of the Founder of Christianity, not as he had uttered them, but according to their own views. These narratives were favorable to the Law of the Jews and to the Jews themselves, when they emanated from the Judeo-Christians, and inimical towards both in the accounts written by the followers of Paul, the Heathen-Christians. The evangelists were thus polemical writers.

Many pagans had initially chosen to convert to Judaism but when the alternative of Christianity and its promise of absolution and redemption became available, (and its elimination of circumcision) some of these pagans who had converted to Judaism now adopted Christianity. Others of these converts chose to reject the concept of a Christian messiah and remain Jewish. One of the oldest prayers in the Jewish liturgy is the Aleinu prayer which might have had its origins as a pledge of fidelity to Judaism and rejection of Christianity. The prayer in the *Sabbath and Festival Prayer Book* (The Rabbinical Assembly of America and the United Synagogue of America, published 1946) reads, in part:

> It is for us to praise the Lord of all, to proclaim the greatness of the Creator of the universe for He hath not made us like the pagans of the world, nor placed us like the heathen tribes of the earth; He hath not made our destiny as theirs, nor cast our lot with all their multitude. We bend the knee, worship and give thanks unto the King of kings, the Holy One, blessed be He.

This prayer seems more like a fraternity pledge than a prayer. It possibly was the Judeo Christians' reaction to the tension between the Heathen Christians and themselves.

In the fourth century as Christianity took hold, conditions got worse for the Jews and they were increasingly isolated and demonized. But rather than lure Jews into conversion to Christianity, this very isolation and demonization served to force the Jews into increasingly insular camps which left them no alternative but to remain Jewish.

Rabbinical political thought now became deeply cautious and conservative and the concept of a messiah became more abstract, and remote. But yet, as historian Shmuel Katz writes, even after the disastrous Bar-Kokhba revolt,

> Jewish life remained active and productive. Banished from Jerusalem, it now centered on Galilee. Refugees returned; Jews who had been sold into slavery were redeemed. In the centuries after Bar Kochba and Hadrian, some of the most significant creations of the Jewish spirit were produced in Palestine. It was there that the Mishnah was completed and the Jerusalem Talmud was compiled.

DEMONIZATION

Judaism now found itself increasingly in the precarious situation of a minority that was considered a dissident sect. PBS Frontline's report chronicles the development of Christianity:

> Over 30 years, Paul clocked up around 10,000 miles, traveling across the Roman Empire. He preached in some of the empire's most important cities. Although places like Ephesus, Philippi, Corinth and Athens looked magnificent, they were also home to tens of thousands of poor, desperate people who were the perfect audience for the Christian message of eternal life.
>
> Like Jesus, Paul spoke to people in their homes and synagogues. But he went beyond Jesus, who had only preached to Jews. Paul believed his message should also be taken to gentiles — the non-Jews.
>
> This meant taking a more relaxed approach to ancient Jewish laws about food and circumcision. It was a slap in the face for Jewish tradition, but it was also the central reason for the rapid spread of Christianity.
>
> As the Christian movement began to accept non-Jewish members, it moved further away from the strict rules imposed on Jews. In so doing, it gradually became a new and separate religion.

UNRV's[21] description of Christianity's efforts to lure the pagans further clarifies the early successes of Christianity after Paul: Early Christians, facing scorn at best and persecution at worst, depending on Emperor and the era, were forced attempted to blend in with their pagan counterparts.

> In order to celebrate the 'holidays' of their religion, the Christians used pre-existing holidays and festivals to blend in. Christmas, for example, was originally part of the great festival of the Winter Solstice, or the Saturnalia. By adopting this grand event as the celebration of Christ's birth, Christian revelry was allowed to take place, largely unnoticed. The Church too manipulated customs and traditions of the Pagan Empire to make their faith more adaptable. One of the more difficult challenges was simply getting people to believe in a single god, and give up all the others that they were accustomed to. In overcoming this obstacle, the Church began to adopt Patron Saints of various daily life functions, to allow an easier conversion. Though these Saints weren't gods in the Pagan sense, having multiple choices for the population to look to for guidance helped ease the transition. The idea of the holy trinity too, harkens to a time

---

21   United Nations of Roma Victrix website aims to give visitors a substantial look into what Rome was.

where people needed separate entities to spread their prayer. Even the office of the Pope as the head of the faith began to replace the Emperor in the eyes of the people as the living incarnation of God on earth.

As the influence of the Catholic Church grew within the Roman Empire, Judaism became the object of severe restrictions at the hands of the legislators. The Jews came to be described as a baleful, disreputable, sacrilegious, perverse, and abominable people.

But through it all, Judaism remained a legally recognized religion, and the emperors, even the least tolerant, ordered that Judaism be respected. The rabbis and dignitaries of the synagogues were placed on the same level with the members of the Catholic clergy. They were made titular heads of their communities, exempted from all burdensome services, from all contributions of forced labor, and they were given the right to expel those who they considered "false brothers" from their communities[22].

At the start of the fifth century, in a further effort at isolation and demonization, the Jews were not permitted to be members of the police or the treasury or be employed in any other public capacity. Jews were prohibited from spreading their religion, especially to the detriment of Christianity and although the preservation and maintenance of the old synagogues was permitted, the erection of new synagogues was prohibited. Marriage with Christian women was prohibited, as was the conversion of free Christians to the Jewish religion[23]. Jews were now required to conform in their marriages to the Roman laws[24]. All disputes that were not strictly religious in character were subject to the Roman law. The parties concerned in the disputes were still entitled to submit their case to the decision of their rabbi if they wished to do so; but this decision, whenever it conflicted with that of the governor, had only the value of simple arbitration

Although these measures were designed to induce numerous conversions, their primary effect was to pen up Judaism, both physically and

---

22 It was this unique power, more than any other, which characterized the Jewish communities throughout the world for the next millennium.

23 The very presence of these laws emphasizes the continuing attractiveness of Judaism to the general population.

24 This gave rise to two wedding marriages with civil ceremonies in addition to religious ceremonies, much the same as today's practice.

morally, forcing Jews within the religion to remain Jewish, and encumbering them with the humiliation and infamy which they were to bear throughout the Middle Ages.

There is no evidence of a sudden Jewish increase in the Christian population. Christianity's growth was clearly related to the growth of the Roman Empire and its success in converting Roman pagans. Although the government expressed a desire for Jewish apostasy, intercourse between Jews and Christians was so limited that this was very unlikely. Because they had been so isolated there very simply was no forum, no opportunity for Jews to convert to Christianity. Any contact between the Jewish and Christian communities was so long distance and so strained that the likelihood of the seduction of large numbers of Jews into Christianity was remote.

THE GROWTH OF RABBINIC JUDAISM

Judaism had experienced a complete change of fortune during the first few centuries of the Common Era. It started out as the religion of choice for the emerging Roman intellectual middle class. And, within just a few centuries it went from religion of choice to anathema. The factor that caused that change was the arrival on the scene of Jesus Christ and his apostle Paul. In the years prior to Christianity, Judaism had been the only truly "spiritual" religion in the Roman world; there was simply no alternative. The combination of a religion organized around the principal of one God along with the humanitarian traditions of Judaism made it an attractive alternative to paganism. The weekly Sabbath and the rituals surrounding it were especially compelling, as was the mythology of the Bible.

But the Christians had a more attractive product and many of the Roman pagans who had been tempted to become Jewish switched their allegiance to Christianity. In reaction to the Christians' successful proselytizing, and in an effort to avoid the weakening of Judaism through dilution, the rabbis began erecting boundaries around Judaism seeking to make it more exclusive and making it more difficult for pagans to convert into Judaism. As a result, as Christianity became more popular, Judaism became more insular. In the fourth century Christianity became the official religion of the Roman Empire. Jews and Christians, who had initially been divergent sects of Judaism, went their separate ways and eventually arrived at positions that were adversarial and far removed from their common heritage. The Christians emphasized their spirituality, the Jews, their scholastics. According to the *Jewish Encyclopedia*:

> The breadth of view and the larger knowledge were now on the side of the Christian, while in the narrow ghetto, the mind of the Jew had become cramped, and his whole life and thought were circumscribed by the Talmud. It was frequently from sincere pity that Christian statesmen and religious leaders looked for the day when, as the Church believed, "the veil of Moses" would be taken from the Jewish people, so that they should no longer appear "as a mere wreck and ruin of the past, a mummy preserved by the centuries only to testify to the living truths of Christianity."

The new rabbinic Jews claimed the higher intellectual ground. The Mishna, they said, had been orally transmitted by God to Moses on Mount Sinai. They called it *Torah she B'al Peh*, the oral Torah.

After the destruction of the Temple and the subsequent expulsion and Diaspora, the rabbis were forced to face a new reality — Judaism without a central authority. There was a flurry of legal discourse following the realization that the old Temple-based system of sacrifice could not be maintained. And so, during this period, historic rabbinic discussions and pronouncements began to be recorded in writing. In the year 200 Rabbi Judah ha-Nassi organized these discussions by subject matter, and this new volume, called the Mishnah, became the dominant starting point for the new Jewish ritual. In the three centuries following the redaction of the Mishnah, rabbis in Jerusalem and Babylonia analyzed, debated and discussed that work. These discussions became the core of the Talmud. The rules of Jewish law and practice that grew out of the Talmud were called Halacha. These laws were assembled as the Mishneh Torah in the twelfth century by Maimonides and were codified as the Shulchan Aruch in the sixteenth century by Rabbi Yosef Karo.

From the second century on, the new Jewish religious leaders promoted the study and reading of the Tanach[25], the Mishna[26], and the Tal-

---

25 An acronym for Torah (Pentateuch), Neviim (Prophets), and Ketuvim (Apocrypha)

26 The codification of Jewish Oral Law

mud[27]. They elevated the status of teachers and scholars, encouraged the construction of synagogues and schools, and *degraded* the status of illiterate people. Literacy skills were rewarded both socially and economically within the new Jewish communities. Those Jews who were able to be scholars moved up the socio-economic ladder while the less literate fell by the wayside.

The following Aramaic prayer, Yakum Purkan, one of the oldest prayers in the Sabbath liturgy, is for the reward of Jewish scholars:

> Heavenly Father, we invoke Thy divine aid upon the scholars and teachers associated in the study of Torah in the land of Israel, in Babylon, and in all the lands of the dispersion. We pray also for those leaders who spread learning among the people, the leaders of the community, those who head schools of learning as well as those who exercise authority in the courts of sacred law. May they, their disciples, the disciples of their disciples and all who apply themselves in the study of the Torah be granted heavenly salvation. Bestow upon them grace, loving-kindness and mercy, long life, ample sustenance, health of body and enlightenment of the mind. May they be blessed with children who will not neglect the Torah. May the ruler of the universe bless them, prolong their lives, increase their days, and add to their years. May they be saved and delivered from every trouble and misfortune. May the Lord of heaven be their help at all times and seasons.

By the fifth century Halacha was firmly entrenched as the principle source for the new Jewish ritual that was being promulgated by the rabbis. Judaism was becoming a religion of written rules and regulations and Jews were becoming the people of the book. As for the Sadducees, and the Samaritans, and the Jewish Hellenists, and the Jewish Christians, and the other groups, they faded away.

It is hard for us to imagine such an exclusionary community, but to get a full idea of the changes that had occurred within the Jewish community we must remember that at the time of the destruction of the Temple in 70 C.E. there was no Talmud, there was no Mishna, there was no "oral tradition", there were no formal prayers, there was no Halachah, no synagogues, no cantors, no liturgy, and such rabbis as existed were scholars, not spiritual leaders. In fact, the Judaism of the fifth century C.E. would have been unrecognizable and probably unacceptable to the Jews who lived before the destruction of the Temple. Most Jewish ritual which we now identify as basic to Judaism didn't exist in the time of the

---

27 Discussion of, and refinement of the Mishna.

Temple. For example, although male Jews were circumcised, the circumcision ritual as we know it wasn't fully developed until its codification in the Mishna, and the bar mitzvah ritual wouldn't be developed until the middle ages. In short, during the time of the Temple, you could be a Jew without doing anything Jewish other than being born into a Jewish household.

Jews did not "join" a synagogue before the Common Era — there were no synagogues per se! Jews did not have to demonstrate their commitment to Halachah — there was no Halachah! Jews did not study Talmud, or Mishna, or the writings of the great sages like Hillel — the Mishna and the Talmud weren't written until after the destruction of the Second Temple, and Hillel was a contemporary philosopher whose writings were not yet considered sacred or venerable. Sure there had been Jewish scholars, and Jewish writings, and Jewish activists and Jewish religious leaders before the Common Era, but the Jews of the Temple years were as much a political body as a religious body, and the spiritual leader was the High Priest.

With the destruction of the Temple and the exile of nearly the entire Jewish population, Judaism had lost its anchor. There was no place to make sacrifices, and there was no sacred ground on which the Jews could congregate. Without the development of rabbinic Judaism, the Jewish religion would certainly have disappeared.

But there was no model for the rabbis to follow — nothing to pattern the new Judaism on. No other religion preached belief in one god. No other religion had a house of worship that was not an enormous temple. No other religion had a central written document like the Torah. No other religion rewarded scholarship. There was no established ritual, no established prayers, and no synagogue service. All of that had to be developed.

It would take a cadre of scholars three hundred years to develop most of what we call Judaism today. Scholarship was the necessary ingredient and scholars were highly respected and well rewarded monetarily. The most brilliant works of the scholars were studied and quoted throughout the Diaspora and the written records of their study and discussions became the Mishna and the Talmud — the backbone of the new Judaism. The discussions, decisions and pronouncements of this elite few and their acolytes became the new core of the Jewish religion.

As Judaism became more scholarly and more insular its members formed into a tightly knit society that was centered on the rabbi and the houses of prayer and study[28]. As a result of this relationship between education and Judaism, Jews typically invested more than non-Jews in their children's education. But as this process continued, it often became a case of diminishing return on investment.

Investing in their own and their children's religious education was costly and not always immediately profitable as there were only a limited number of leadership positions available in the community. Eventually, a large proportion of Jews chose to leave the community rather than submit to the ultimately unrewarding educational pressures. As this population left, the per capita costs and requisite maintenance of the remaining community became more of a burden for its remaining constituents. The Jews who stayed with the new rabbinic Judaism became the core of Judaism and were counted as Jews. The more secular and non scholarly Jews were often cast out and defamed by the rabbinic community and were not counted by the rabbis as part of the Jewish community, although they remained Jews.

In today's terms the Jews within the rabbinic community might be called *affiliated*, the others, *unaffiliated*.

Here's how Abba Eban, former Israeli Ambassador to the United States, brilliantly described the typical rabbinic Jewish community in his commentary on the totality of the Jewish experience, *My People, The Story of the Jews*, (Behrman House, New York, 1968, p. 215):

> [T]he synagogue was the hub and nucleus of communal life, together with the schools connected to it. Indeed, intensive education, at all levels, was the distinctive and controlling feature of Jewish life. It was not an abstract, academic truth which scholars of the ghetto sought in their studies; they lived by the teaching they pored over in the academy. Talmudism, as the Jew felt it, meant a preoccupation with existential reality, not a denial of it. The thousands of communal regulations issued by the great medieval rabbis represented the fruits of an ongoing adjustment of legal norms and precepts to the conditions surrounding the Jew in his new world.

---

28   The Yiddish word for synagogue is shul which literally means school.

[A]side from synagogues and schools, the Jews had their own courts and administrative offices. Occasionally they even achieved the dignity of a town hall. They had communal baths, bakeries, slaughter-houses, inns, cemeteries, and even prisons, administered by their own elected authorities. The government of the community was vested in a body of *parnasim* (leaders), usually numbering twelve in the larger centers. One of these, as a rule the rabbi, was recognized by the secular authorities as the responsible head of the Jewry, often called the Jew's Bishop.

The Jews in these rabbinic communities had to live in a district that was large enough to support a kosher butcher (shochet), a house of prayer, a mikva[29], a school, and a residence for the rabbi. This required that the community become as insular and self sufficient as possible. Although there were many demands made on the members of the community, the rewards were limited to a few of the brightest and/or best connected.

Today, we can still see the powerful insularity of these communities. Rather than be identified by their unique religious philosophy, many of today's ultra orthodox communities choose to be called by the ancient European town in which they had flourished. Dynasties like the Satmar who originally come from the city of Satu Mare, in present-day Romania; the Belz from the town of Belz in Western Ukraine; the Bobov which originated in Bobowa, Galicia in Southern Poland; the Ger from Ger (the Yiddish name of Góra Kalwaria), a small town in Poland; the Munkatch of the Hungarian town of Munkacs; and the Vizhnitz, a Hasidic dynasty from Vyzhnytsia, a village in present-day Ukraine, to name but a few that retain their geographical ties. One of the largest of these communities is the Skver Hasidic dynasty which was founded by Rebbe Yitzchok Twerski in the city of Skver in present-day Ukraine. There is currently one main off-shoot of the Skverer dynasty. It is led by Grand Rabbi David Twersky and is headquartered in New Square (often pronounced "New Skver"), New York. A recent scandal in the community provides an example of the hold that the rabbis still exert in these insular rabbinic communities.

As reported by Peter Applebome in the *New York Times* on June 6th, 2011:

Last September, Aron Rottenberg did something radical.

---

29 Ritual bath.

Along with some friends, he began worshiping not at the grand synagogue at the center of this ultra-Orthodox Skver Hasidic community in Rockland County, but outside the village at a residence for the elderly.

Before long, a rabbinical court ruled that praying outside the synagogue was a serious violation of community rules.

Next, groups outside Mr. Rottenberg's house smashed windows and dumped his daughter's school desk and books on the front porch. And on May 22, an early-morning attack left Mr. Rottenberg with third-degree burns over most of his body.

Shaul Spitzer, 18, who lived in the house of Grand Rabbi David Twersky and worked as his butler, was charged with attempted murder and attempted arson. Mr. Spitzer, too, was hospitalized with serious burns.

[Grand Rabbi Twersky, 70, who has led New Square and Skverer Hasidim worldwide, since his father died in April 1968, issued a statement four days after the attack in which he said he was praying for Mr. Rottenberg's recovery.

"We condemn in the strongest possible terms the use of violence under any circumstances," he said.

The Rottenberg family had recently installed surveillance cameras out of fear of attacks and harassment. Mr. Rottenberg's eldest son, Jacob, was monitoring the cameras around 4 a.m. on May 22 when he saw at least one intruder placing gasoline-soaked rags behind the house. Screaming, he awoke his father, who ran outside only to have the gasoline explode and set him afire.

Mr. Spitzer was ordered held on $300,000 bail during his arraignment at the burn unit of New York-Presbyterian Hospital/Weill Cornell Medical Center in Manhattan, where he has been treated for burns to his arms and hands.

[Police] records show that the Rottenberg family had reported increasing threats and attacks since mid-September, when Mr. Rottenberg and some friends began praying at the residence for the elderly. Mr. Rottenberg has since said he started to do so because a friend there was being treated for cancer.

The Journal News, a newspaper Mr. Rottenberg visited in November, saying he feared for his safety, reported Sunday that violence in the community was the result of gangs of young zealots intent on supporting the rabbi.

NEWLY UNAFFILIATED

History is always written by the victor, or in this case, by the surviving sect. So our knowledge of Jewish history, from around the fifth century forward is based on the histories recorded by the Pharisees and their rabbinic descendants. The rabbis who wrote the Talmud and Halacha, and all of their sister and daughter writings became the new core of the Jewish people; and the Sadducees, and the Hellenistic Jews, and the Samaritans who had fought against the new (rabbinic) Judaism, were now in the dust bin of the forgotten and forgettable past.

There were many needs in the new rabbinic communities. Schools had to be organized, teachers had to be trained, synagogues had to be built, ritual had to be created and prayers had to be written. But the responsibility for filling those needs was limited to a few of the brightest and/or best connected. The rest of the rabbinic community's population was relegated to menial community maintenance tasks[30]. The main need in the new rabbinic Jewish communities was for scholars and poets and visionaries and these special people were amply rewarded both monetarily and in public esteem.

Only about twenty five percent of the Jews who lived during the first few centuries of the Common Era chose to join the rabbinic communities. The limited opportunities that these communities offered for the non-scholarly population and their restrictive environment resulted in the disaffection and defection[31] of more than 75% of the early Diaspora Jews.

What happened to these Jews who chose not to compete in the scholarship race of the rabbinic community?

The most widely offered answer is that they converted to Christianity. But historically, that is not at all likely. The Christian Church, which offered an attractive alternative to paganism, was growing so rapidly and achieving such strength and influence among the Romans that they had no need or desire for Jews to join their Church. And, from the fifth century on, the Christian community had so isolated and demonized the Jews that they were not welcome, even as converts.

---

30 Like Tevye, the milkman in the "Fiddler" stories.
31 Another way to look at this is to imagine that in the absence of the Temple ritual most Jews chose not to join the rabbinic communities.

The unaffiliated Jews who had been estranged from the Jewish community sought opportunities in the outside world wherever they were offered. Eventually, because they were more mobile, and because they maintained their loose social and commercial ties to other Jews, and because they were willing to do what the Church had forbidden[32], they became merchants and bankers. And as markets spread further afield, they followed. Some became the agents of the landowners, typically performing the unpleasant tasks of land management and enforcement. Some became peddlers, or entertainers, or itinerant doctors. They worked as day laborers, or messengers, or small merchants, or traders, or, in later years, as bankers and teachers and musicians. And some families quietly amassed fortunes and eventually became the engines of the Enlightenment and the sponsors of the Industrial Revolution. They self identified as Jews but, given the virulent anti Semitism of the middle ages, they tried, wherever possible, to blend in with the community in which they were living. Whereas the rabbinic Jews were umbilically attached to their rabbi and their community and their religion, the unaffiliated Jews were assimilated and as difficult to find as chameleons.

The apocryphal and unlikely story of Esther[33] that is the basis of the Purim holiday is an example of this existence. In it, Esther enters a beauty contest and is chosen to be the new queen, but she is reluctant to reveal her Jewish identity for fear of rejection. So she "passes" until circumstances force her to declare her Jewish roots. When she finally does reveal her Jewish identity, she does so with great trepidation. The reward for her overcoming this risk is the salvation of the entire Jewish community.

The Roman Empire and the Ottoman Empire offered fertile ground for adventurous Jewish men. They traveled to the furthest reaches of the empire to manage the commerce of staples as well as new and highly valued material. Many of them worked along the silk route, which ran through Bukhara and Tashkent all the way east nearly to the Pacific Ocean; or the spice route which ran from Arabia through India, to China.

---

32 Specifically banking and various forms of commerce which involved extending credit.

33 The Book of Esther can be found in the Apocrypha (Ketuvim) section of the Tanach.

They went wherever opportunities presented themselves and there were many opportunities in the rapidly growing Roman and Ottoman empires. They traveled alone or with caravans all over the known world; and they settled and established outposts and trading centers along the routes[34].

They probably married non-Jews whom they purchased as brides as was the custom of the time. These non-Jewish brides became, by virtue of their marriage, Jewish[35]. And, by the rules of maternal descent, even though the wives of these Jewish adventurers were not born Jewish, their descendants were. The fact that there is a large racial diversity in today's Jewish community and that Jews in each country tend to resemble their host community physically is because the founding mothers of these small Jewish communities were local women. The strong presence and commitment of the Jewish patriarchs combined with the later stigmatization of Jews explains why a surprisingly large minority of these families remained Jewish.

When a particular host country threatened their existence, or when they perceived an opportunity elsewhere, they moved on, always seeking a better life. They continued to live wherever opportunity presented itself. They married Jews whenever possible and they married non-Jews when necessary. Only the strongest and wiliest were able to succeed in this often hostile environment, and only the most determined were able to retain their Jewish identity. Nicholas Wade writing on these far flung Jewish outposts in *The New York Times* (May 14, 2002) reported that recent DNA studies show that the Jewish men in these locations were genetically related to one another and to present-day Middle Eastern populations, but not to the men of the communities in which they lived.

> The finding suggested that Jewish men who founded the communities traced their lineage back to the ancestral Mideastern population of 4,000 years ago from which Arabs, Jews and other people are descended. It pointed to the genetic unity of widespread Jewish populations and took issue with ideas that most Jewish communities were relatively recent converts like the Khazars, a medieval Turkish tribe that embraced Judaism.

---

34 These merchants were similar to the Jewish peddlers who established towns and department stores throughout rural America.

35 According to Shaya Cohen, "the woman was joined to the house of Israel by being joined to her Israelite husband; the act of marriage was functionally equivalent to the later act of 'conversion'" (p. 265 The Beginnings of Jewishness)

Interestingly, another study by Dr. David Goldstein, Dr. Mark Thomas and Dr. Neil Bradman of University College in London and other colleagues, which appears in The American Journal of Human Genetics shows that the women in nine Jewish communities from Georgia in the former Soviet republic, to Morocco have completely different genetic histories from the men. This indicates that the community had very few founding mothers and that after the community was founded there was very little mixture with the host population. Unlike the case with the men, the women's identities are not related to one another or to those of present-day Middle Eastern populations.

Dr. Goldstein, the lead author of the study speculated that most Jewish communities were formed by unions between Jewish men and local women.

> "The men came from the Near East, perhaps as traders," he said. "They established local populations, probably with local women. But once the community was founded, the barriers had to go up, because otherwise mitochondrial diversity would be increased." (italics mine)

This thesis, that most or all Jewish communities were founded by Jewish men who originated in the Middle East and local women is somewhat at variance with the usual founding traditions in which it is claimed that they were formed by families who fled persecution or were invited to settle by local kings.

For example, the Iraqi Jewish community claims to be descended from exiles to Babylon after the destruction of the First Temple in 586 B.C. And members of the Bene Israel community in India say that they are the children of Jews who fled the persecutions of Antiochus Epiphanus, around 150 B.C.E.

Dr. Shaye Cohen, professor of Jewish literature and philosophy at Harvard, said the conclusions drawn from the genetic study, and the implications that Jewish communities were founded by traders, was "by no means implausible."

> "The authors are correct in saying the historical origins of most Jewish communities are unknown," Dr. Cohen said. "Not only the little ones like in India, but even the mainstream Ashkenazic culture from which most American Jews descend."

But these itinerant Jews and their families had no core — no magnetic center that would keep them from eventually losing their Jewish identity. And so they seized the opportunity, when it presented itself, to join an existing Jewish community or to form a new one of their own. As can be imagined, these outsiders often presented problems of integration within the insular rabbinic communities which led to fragmentation, and the establishment of competing congregations[36].

A large percentage of these unaffiliated Jews eventually converted to Christianity, but nearly as large a percentage remained faithful to Judaism. Some (involuntarily) straddled the line. Consider the following biography of Antonio Ribeiro Sanchez as reported in the Jewish Encyclopedia:

> [Antonio Ribeiro Sanchez was a] Russian court physician; born 1699; died in Paris 1783; member of a Marano family of Penamacor, district of Castello Branca, Portugal. Sanchez, with many coreligionists, escaped from the persecutions in Portugal and went to Holland, where he studied medicine at the University of Leyden. There he enjoyed the friendship of his professor, the eminent physician Herman Boerhaave, who formed a very high opinion of Sanchez's ability. When Empress Anna Ivanovna of Russia requested Boerhaave (1731) to send her a learned physician who would be competent to act as her medical adviser, he recommended Sanchez, who entered her service the same year. The empress was so pleased with Sanchez that she appointed him chief physician of the Cadets; and soon after he was elected member of the Imperial Academy of Science. In 1740, after the death of Anna Ivanovna, Sanchez was appointed, by the regent Anna Leopoldovna, physician to the young prince Ivan Antonovich. She had such confidence in him that even from Riga she sent to him for examination the prescriptions of the attending physicians.
>
> At this time Sanchez had a large practice and many influential friends in St. Petersburg. He devoted his leisure hours to study, and accumulated a valuable collection of medical works. When the regency of Anna Leopoldovna ended, in 1741, and many statesmen and courtiers were replaced, Sanchez was retained as physician to the empress Elizabeth Petrovna. He enjoyed her favor and maintained his reputation as one of the most skilful physicians in Europe. In 1744, Sanchez attended the princess Sophia Augusta, afterward Empress Catherine II., and, according to the statement in her "Memoirs," saved her from a dangerous illness. He was then elevated to the rank of councilor of state.

---

36 The humorous anecdote about the Jew who is stranded on a desert island and builds two synagogues, "the one I attend and the one I wouldn't set foot in," is reminiscent of this divisive tradition.

Three years later Sanchez was suddenly ordered to resign and to leave St. Petersburg. Officially he received his conge on account of illness. In the acceptance of his resignation Elizabeth praises (*sic*) his great skill as a physician and the honesty with which he had discharged his duties. Sanchez's dismissal astonished the court circle, especially as he was known never to have interfered in politics. He hastened to sell his property, and then went to Paris. His library, purchased by the empress, greatly enriched the medical department of the imperial library. The mystery of his dismissal gave Sanchez no rest, and soon after his arrival in Paris he wrote to the president of the Imperial Academy of Science, Count K. G. Razumovski, asking for an explanation. The latter, in turn, wrote to the chancellor Bestyuzhev; and from both letters it appears that the only reason for Sanchez's discharge was the fact that the empress, who hated the Jews, had been told that he professed JudaWhen Sanchez learned this he resigned himself to the situation, and again devoted himself to the study and practice of medicine. He became very popular in the poorer quarters of Paris; but work among the poor, whom he treated gratuitously, ruined both his health and his finances. Some of the Russian dignitaries, who corresponded with him, considered it their duty to aid him; and Catherine II was induced to grant him a life pension of 1,000 rubles annually (1762).

Sanchez was the first medical writer to acquaint the physicians of Europe with the medical value of the Russian vapor-baths, through his work "De Cura Variolarum Vaporarii Ope apud Russos" (Russian transl. "O Parnykh Rossiskikh Banyakh," St. Petersburg, 1779). He was the author also of "Sur l'Origine de la Maladie Venerienne" (On the Origin of Venereal Disease) (Lisbon, 1750).

During the years that the rabbinic scholars had relatively safe and stable Jewish communities in which to do their studying and make their contribution, their production of important works was prodigious. For example, the stable Jewish communities in the Moslem empire which included modern day Spain, Morocco, Yemen, and Syria gave rise to brilliant scholars like Saadia Gaon in Iraq, who was the first important rabbinic figure to write extensively in Arabic and produced a rational investigation of the contents of the Bible; David Ibn Marw□n al-Mukammas al-Rakki in Syria who was the author of the earliest known Jewish philosophical work of the Middle Ages; Samuel Ha-Nagid, a brilliant teacher and scholar, Solomon ibn Gabirol, an early highly recognized philosopher, Abraham bar-Hiyya Ha-Nasi, author of "Meditation of the Soul", an ethical work written from a rationalistic religious viewpoint, Bahya ben Joseph ibn Paquda, author of the first Jewish system of ethics and Yehuda Ha-Levi who wrote about his views of Judaism relative to other religions of the time were all from Spain; and the brilliant Rambam (Maimonodes) who wrote "The Guide for the Perplexed" lived in Morocco.

But after the expulsion from Spain and the collapse of the Ottoman Empire, the rabbinic Jews were not able to settle in any country long enough for the new community to become established. When they did find a hospitable settling place, they spent most of their initial energy rebuilding the communal infrastructure, and less on scholarly pursuits. It was only after the infrastructure of synagogue, school and support system was established in these new communities that the scholars were able to turn their attention to theological matters. Consequently, the period between the expulsion from Spain in the fifteenth century and the establishment of rabbinic communities in Poland some three centuries later produced fewer notable scholars.

While the rabbinic Jews were struggling to produce scholars, the Jews who had left the rabbinic communities were producing merchants and bankers and adventurers who were establishing their own communities all across the known world. And as the Jewish communal situation changed, the advantage shifted to the unaffiliated Jews. Rabbinic Jewish scholarly writings of the time are filled with laudatory descriptions of scholars, and disparaging references and responses to defection, assimilation and conversion. These themes of denigration of non scholars by the rabbinic community continue to this day.

The Jews who had so highly valued their intellectual and literacy skills a thousand years earlier were still living as they had for the previous millennium, moving and rebuilding their intact communities as necessary. Their population remained stagnant because there was a steady stream of internal selection and reward of the scholars which led to disaffection and consequent disaffiliation.

* * *

Although many of the unaffiliated Jews remained Jews, they were not members of any of the established rabbinic Jewish communities. And so, they were never counted in any of the periodic census counts. Remember, this is before the post office and before any reliable forms of communication. The way a census[37] was managed was that the government asked the leaders of the various communities to count and identify the people within their community. In the case of Jews, the rabbi, who was usually the leader of the community, had a very easy time — all he had to do is count the families that attended services. He knew of every birth and every death, and, because ages and family relationships are very important in Judaism, (every child is known by the name of his/her father) the rabbi had readily available records on the members of his community.

But there were no rabbis to count the Jews who lived where there was no organized Jewish community. Because these Jews probably maintained as low a profile as possible, attempting to blend in with the surrounding population, they tended to keep their religion to themselves and hoped that the surrounding non Jews were not even aware that they were Jewish.

These Jewish men traveled throughout the Roman and Ottoman Empires, seeking business opportunities and establishing small Jewish communities wherever they settled. They became adventurers, and merchants, and even mercenaries. Some remained Jewish, most did not. There is some evidence that the Sadducees, who had opposed the establishment of rabbinic Judaism after the destruction of the Temple, and who had lost the fight for the control of Judaism were among these unaffiliated Jews. The theory is that after their defeat by the Pharisees, they had traveled north and east from Jerusalem, and settled on the shores of the Black Sea where they established what eventually became Karaite communities. The Jewish Encyclopedia (adapted) writes that:

> [about] the time that Greek and Roman culture began to influence the northern portion of Africa the Jews began to spread into these regions; indeed, they went even beyond the confines of the Roman Empire. Egypt, according to the testimony of Philo, was inhabited, as far as the borders of Libya and Ethiopia, by Jews whose numbers were estimated at a million. The great mercantile city of Alexandria was the intellectual and commercial center of African Jewish life. Alexander the Great had conferred upon the Jews full rights of citizenship, and they guarded these rights jealously. In Cyrene [Libya] also they were of importance; and their progress may be traced by the aid of inscriptions as far as Volubilis, [Morocco] in the

---

37 The primary purposes of the census during the middle ages was for conscription and taxation, both of which, the unaffiliated sought to avoid.

extreme west of Mauretania.[North Africa] [A]ccording to Jerome[38], the Jews dwelt in a continuous chain of settlements, from Mauretania eastward, throughout the province of Africa, and in Palestine, reaching as far as India. If they were interrogated on Biblical matters they gave no answer, probably in order to avoid being drawn into disputes with Christians. [Judaism] in these regions did not dissolve or merge into Christianity; on the contrary, it continued to maintain its independent existence.

POPULATION EXPLOSION

During the centuries following the establishment of the first rabbinic communities, the official world Jewish population declined. Through success and failure, invitations and expulsions, poverty and prosperity the known Jewish population slowly and inexorably declined.

And then starting in 1750, nearly two thousand years after the beginning of rabbinic Judaism, the world Jewish population soared. In the years from 1750 to the Holocaust, while the general world population grew 300%, the world Jewish population grew 1600%! *More than five time the world's growth rate.*

Where did all those Jews come from?

Actually, they were always there. The Jews never disappeared in the first five hundred years of the Common Era, nor did they magically appear in the last two centuries. They were always there, or at least a fairly substantial portion of them: Hidden in plain sight. The reason for the apparent loss and gain of Jewish population was within Judaism itself. Through a combination of self selection and necessity, the new rabbinic Jewish community had created two clearly defined classes of Jews: Affiliated, and unaffiliated. The affiliated Jews became the core of rabbinic Judaism. The unaffiliated Jews eventually became disenfranchised, and ultimately departed organized rabbinic Judaism. From the beginning of the rabbinic period until the start of the eighteenth century, *only the affiliated Jews were counted by the Jewish community.*

---

38   Also known as Sophronius, Jerome was a medieval church scholar, first a hermit and then a secretary to Pope Damasus in the 380s. From there he went to Palestine and devoted himself to study and writing. He wrote ecclesiastical histories, exegeses and translations, and is credited with shaping the Latin version of the Bible (called the Vulgate) from Hebrew and Greek texts.

Almost from the beginning, as the Jews adjusted to their exile and the loss of the Temple in Jerusalem, the Romans recognized the rabbis as the leaders of their communities. In return for population management and tax collection, the Romans granted the rabbis all sorts of secular powers among which were governmental representation, and internal judicial and religious control. The new rabbinic Jewish community was taxed by the Roman government in the same manner as every other community[39] and the rabbis were responsible for the maintenance of population records and the collection of taxes. The Jews who remained within the rabbinic communities were counted and taxed as Roman citizens; those who had left the community were not. Thus, those Jews who, for various reasons, were not part of the rabbinic community, ceased to exist from a statistical point of view.

The lives of these "wandering Jews" contrasted greatly with the lives of the village-based rabbinic Jews. The wandering Jews did not have to build a synagogue, did not have to establish a yeshiva, and did not have to have a mikva or a kosher butcher, or a matzo bakery. They lived by their wits and adapted to their environment. And when that environment became hostile, they moved on to another, more hospitable environment. They were variously called assimilated Jews or crypto Jews or Marranos or apikorsim[40], and they were increasingly disparaged by the rabbinic establishment.

The world's ever present hostility, the need to assimilate; to "pass," the constant fear of discovery, and especially their lack of personal identity, weighed heavily on the unaffiliated Jews. Although they were reasonably successful on the world's commercial stage, they had no distinctiveness and no affiliation[41]. And, as can be seen from the story in the preceding chapter about Antonio Ribeiro Sanchez, even when they assimilated on the highest levels, they could never quite shed their Jewish identity. The age of enlightenment was beginning, and the Jews wanted to be part of Europe's awakening, but to do that they had to come out of the shadows.

---

39 In the 4th century an additional tax was imposed on the Jewish communities
40 non-believers
41 Sir Walter Scott's passionate poem "Patriotism" beautifully articulates this yearning. (see appendix)

Toward the end of the eighteenth century the unaffiliated Jews finally saw an opportunity to shed their anonymity. Timidly at first and then with greater temerity, and defiance, they declared their Jewishness. The Age of Enlightenment with its opportunities for equal education and academic competition had opened the door a crack and the Jews poured through. In the next few chapters we will see how the Academies, and the Learned Societies, the Republic of Letters, the Coffee Houses and Cafes, the Debating Societies, and especially the Salons, gave these worldly Jews a platform from which, *as Jews*, they could expound their philosophy, learn of the teachings and writings of others, and discuss and share their experiences and knowledge.

They finally had a public platform which they did not have to avoid because of their religion, and they finally were able to claim the respect that their heritage of adventure and investigation had earned.

In their hearts many of these unaffiliated Jews wanted to become affiliated — to rejoin the Jewish community; but on their terms. The rabbinic communities had become too restrictive, too elitist, and too disparaging of *religiously* uneducated Jews. Possibly in reaction to the mistaken acceptance of the false messiah Sabbatai Zevi[42] in the 17th century, the rabbis perceived threats to their control coming from all directions and they became even more insular. The penalties for leaving the community became more severe and the barriers for reentry of lapsed Jews were set ever higher. Even within the rabbinic communities the imposition of absolute control became imperative.

The experience of Baruch Spinoza is a prime example of this exclusionary and elitist attitude.

Baruch Spinoza, also known as Benedict de Spinoza was one of the most important philosophers in the 17th century. He made significant contributions in virtually every area of philosophy.

Spinoza came into the world a Jew. Born in 1632, he was the descendant of a Marrano family who had immigrated to Amsterdam from Por-

---

42 A Sephardic Rabbi and kabbalist who claimed to be, and was initially widely accepted as the long-awaited Jewish Messiah. At the age of forty, he was forced to convert to Islam which was devastating to his followers and was used to show the falsity of his messianic claim.

tugal in order to escape the Inquisition. Spinoza's father, Michael, was a successful merchant and a respected member of the community.

As a young man, Spinoza was educated in his congregation's academy, the Talmud Torah School. There he received instruction in Hebrew, liturgy, Torah, prophetic writings, and rabbinical commentaries. Although Spinoza excelled in these, he did not move on to the higher levels of study which focused on the Talmud and were typically undertaken by those preparing for the rabbinate. Whether by desire or by necessity, Spinoza left the school in order to work in his father's business, which he eventually took over with his half-brother, Gabriel.

Spinoza is best known for his "Ethics," a monumental work in which he talks about the relationship between God and nature. Spinoza believed that God and Nature are synonymous and that rather than think of Nature (and the world) as having been created by God, we should think of God and Nature as being the same.

Spinoza's intellectual achievements came at a cost. His increasingly unorthodox views and, perhaps, laxity in his observance of Jewish law strained his relations with the Jewish community. Tensions became so great that, in 1656, the elders of the synagogue undertook proceedings to excommunicate him. Without providing details, the writ of excommunication accuses him of "abominable heresies" and "monstrous deeds". It then levels a series of curses against him and prohibits others from communicating with him, doing business with him, reading anything he might write, or even coming into close proximity with him. Spinoza may still have been a Jew, but he was now an outcast.

We do not know for certain what Spinoza's "monstrous deeds" and "abominable heresies" were alleged to have been. Little is known about Spinoza's activities in the years immediately following his excommunication. As it was now impossible for him to carry on in commerce, it was most likely at this time that he took up lens grinding as an occupation. He began work on a full presentation of his thoughts in the early 1660s, and by 1665 substantial portions of what was to become the Ethics were circulating in draft form among his friends in Amsterdam. Though he was well into the project by then, the religious climate of the day made Spinoza hesitant to complete it.

Spinoza died peacefully in his rented room in The Hague in 1677. He left no will, only the manuscripts of his unpublished works which included The Treatise on the Emendation of the Intellect, the Ethics, a Hebrew Grammar, and the Political Treatise.

Baruch Spinoza's intellectual achievements had threatened the status quo and the superiority of the rabbis, and he had to be silenced in the most absolute way. It was necessary for the rabbis to maintain a tight control on the religious Jewish population because they perceived that the continued survival of the Jewish people as well as their rabbinic status depended upon it.

And then that control broke down. Surprisingly, the force for that breakdown came initially from within the rabbinic movement. Beginning in the late 1700s and continuing for the next hundred years, three new Jewish movements opened the doors for the reentry of the previously unaffiliated Jews. Exclusionary rabbinic Judaism which had ruled the religion for nearly two thousand years waned and eventually disappeared altogether. Judaism changed to a degree that could not have been anticipated and those Jews who had been living on the outside returned in rapidly increasing numbers. The Hassidic, Mussar, and Haskalah[43] movements, all of which were initiated by rabbis who came from traditional backgrounds opened the doors as never before.

These new movements within the Jewish community enabled the unaffiliated Jews to reenter Jewish society. Their lack of religious skills and Talmudic knowledge which had held them back, were no longer barriers to entry. Now, for the first time, they could point to their long term spiritual dedication, intellectual achievements, and moral commitment to affirm their right to stand among the giants of the Jewish community. Many of the world's most brilliant authors, artists, musicians and philanthropists were Jewish. Many of the bankers and captains of industry were Jewish. And many of the scholars and philosophers and scientists and doctors were Jewish. Now they could proudly reveal their religion.

43　These three movements, and their origins and impact will be discussed in detail in a later chapter

CHALLENGE AND RESPONSE

"Not possible!" is the common reaction that I get when I present this thesis. "It's just not possible for Jews to have wandered off and to have remained Jewish."

Well, most of them did not remain Jewish. Most of them wandered off and intermarried.

If all of the Jews who were alive in the year 500 had remained Jewish, and the Jewish growth rate was the same as the general world growth rate[44], then the Jewish population in the year 1938 would have been 36 million. But it was only 16 million. That disparity, even allowing for pogroms and other murders and persecutions, reflects the fact that more than half of these wandering Jews intermarried and eventually left the faith.

But some of them, enough of them, stayed Jewish.

They lived all over the world constantly pioneering new settlements and new opportunities.

- Jews settled in Algeria in the first centuries of the Common Era, and in the 14th century, with the deterioration of conditions in Spain, many Spanish Jews moved to Algeria.
- Jews have lived in Egypt since biblical times. In 1897 there were more than 25,000 Jews in Egypt.
- Ethiopia is one of the oldest Diaspora communities. It is believed that the Jewish community which calls itself Beta Israel was established in the 2nd or 3rd century C.E.
- The Jews in Libya trace their roots back to the third century.
- The Moroccan Jewish community dates back more than 2,000 years. There were Jewish colonies in Morocco before it became a Roman province. In 1391 there was a new wave of immigration from Spain that brought new life to the community.
- The Jewish presence in Syria dates back to biblical times. Unrest in neighboring Iraq in the 10th century resulted in Jewish migra-

---

44 Typically, because of better sanitation, dietary restrictions, and living conditions (a higher percentage of Jews were urban) Jews had a longer life expectancy that gentiles. This was very apparent during the Black Plague which decimated the general population and spared most of the Jewish population.

tion to Syria and brought about a boon in commerce, banking, and crafts.

- Several sages mentioned in the Talmud lived in Tunisia from the 2nd to the 4th centuries.
- The Jews of Yemen trace their origins back to biblical times. The first recorded reference to Yemenite Jews appears in the 3rd century C.E.
- The Jewish community of Afghanistan can be traced back at least 800 years. In the 12th century there were 80,000 Jews living in the province of Ghazni.
- Myanmar (Burma) had a Jewish population beginning in the early 18th century.
- China had an established Jewish merchant community in the 8th century.
- The Bene Israel claim to have arrived in India in the second century B.C.E. The Cochin community of India, especially the "Black Jews" retain their Jewish identity although they clearly resemble their Indian neighbors. The "Baghdadi Jews" first arrived from Iraq, and Iran around 1796.
- There were Dutch Jews who migrated to Indonesia.
- British Jews who migrated to New Zealand.
- Conversos lived in The Philippines.
- The autochthonous Caucasus Mountain Jews, or Tats, in Azerbaijan, trace their roots back many centuries and speak a Hebrew-tinged dialect.
- Jews have lived in Moldova since the 15th century.
- The Bukharan Jewish community claims descent from 5th century exiles from Persia.

Jacob Silverman, writing about his visit to Kenya in *Tablet Magazine* (March 31, 2011), tells of a man named Yosef Njogu, a slim man with a lively demeanor and a ready smile who comes from Eldoret in western Kenya's Rift Valley province. Eldoret, a town of almost 200,000, is ethnically mixed and is a flashpoint for Kenya's frequent eruptions of ethnic violence.

In Eldoret, Njogu belonged to the Seventh Day of God Adventist Church where members had observed a mixture of observances which fell somewhere between Christian and Jewish beliefs. After a visit by some black Kenyans from Nairobi who had been practicing Judaism, Njogu and several other members of his church decided to commit themselves completely to Judaism.

It's unclear how many black Kenyans practice Judaism. In Njogu's congregation, which includes a few families in the surrounding area, there are about 50 people.

Njogu said that there were a few Jewish families near Nakuru, 30 miles to the west, and they tried to get together with them for major holidays and that in Nairobi, black Kenyans occasionally attend services at the Orthodox synagogue. But that synagogue caters to a mostly expat community that is all white and 80 percent Israeli. Members of the black community, however, had at times felt unwelcome.

Harriet Bograd, who runs Kulanu, the organization that works with isolated or emerging Jewish communities, reported that Njogu's son Samson had been turned away from the Nairobi Hebrew Congregation. Charles Szlapak, the unofficial leader of the Nairobi congregation, said, "I am [aware] that there are places in Kenya where groups of people have decided to call themselves Jewish and even to place a signboard outside a building, calling it a synagogue."

Maggie Jonsson, the Nairobi congregation's community coordinator, said that some black Kenyans prayed at the synagogue—and were welcome. But she avoided the question when asked about their ethnic authenticity or the possibility of their conversion to Judaism. According to Jacob Silverman, "She cited the congregation's lack of resources (they have no permanent rabbi), questioned the motives of those wishing to convert, said that potential converts should study in Israel or the United States, and later declared that just as people can't choose their family members, they should not be allowed to choose their religion. At one point, she allowed that the Nairobi Hebrew Congregation might have to revisit its attitude toward converts if the congregation hopes to survive."

Silverman goes on to say,

In the past, particularly during colonial times, there have been other informal Jewish movements among black Kenyans. According to the Nairobi Hebrew Congregation's official history, *Glimpses of the Jews of Kenya*, the town of Ol Kalou, which is near Gathundia, contains the remnants of "Mt. Zion Synagogue," established by a black community in the pre-independence era. As with many African ethnic groups, particularly in East Africa, the "lost tribe" label sometimes gets tossed around by scholars and even politicians; the Kalenjin and Meru have both been cited as such, the former by Daniel arap Moi, a Kalenjin who was Kenya's second president. The Meru are a Bantu tribe and, like some other Bantu peoples, the Meru have a bit of folklore that describes their escape from bondage under a brown-skinned people and a subsequent flight across a parted body of water referred to as a Red Sea. In Customs and Traditions of the Meru, Daniel Nyaga, a Kenyan scholar, says that he heard the story from multiple people who had had no contact with the Bible.

This is just the tip of the iceberg. There is a large Jewish population in South America that fled there to escape the Inquisition, and every country and city in Europe has had a strong Jewish presence.

And this is just the Jews whose presence is known. There is another, phantom population that still avoids identification. Many of these unaffiliated Jews remain unaffiliated, and under cover. Many of them have intermarried, but many have not. Surprisingly, even today, in the face of religious oppressions in their countries, nearly 2 million Jews from Africa, Asia, and Eurasia have immigrated to Israel. But another million continue to live quietly under the radar in their native countries.

Even in the United States, where religious freedom is the policy of the land, a 2010 study reported in the North American Jewish Data Bank implies that they *just discovered* 1 million formerly unreported (and uncounted) Jews in the United States. The reason for the previous under reporting is, they say, is that they have discovered a new group of Jews who self identify as Jewish, but do not fit into any of the rigidly established categories. In the words of the survey: *"The number of Jews who identify as Jewish by other criteria is almost 975,000."* They do not explain what "Jewish by other criteria" means, but I think it's fair to say that these Jews would fall into the unaffiliated category.

Even within the rabbinic communities there were ongoing defections at nearly the same rate as in the non rabbinic population. If the rabbinic Jewish population growth had kept pace with the world's population growth there should have been 2.7 million rabbinic Jews in the world in 1750[45]. But there were only one million, which means that over the years, even allowing for the oppressions and pogroms, more than half the Jews in the rabbinic communities left Judaism.

* * *

Now that we have established that there were hidden Jews throughout the world who had survived under the radar since the beginning of the Diaspora, it is time to look at what changes occurred in the eighteenth and nineteenth centuries that made it possible for them to resurface and claim their rightful and dominant place in modern Jewish history:

---

45   The Bubonic Plague around 1350 killed an estimated 1/3 of the population of Europe. Jews, for various reasons (cleanliness, rapid burial, dietary restrictions), fared better than the general population and consequently were frequently blamed for the disease

Chapter 2. The Eighteenth and Nineteenth Centuries

The Intellectual Environment

Origins

The incredible changes that the world experienced during the eighteenth and nineteenth centuries had their origins in the transformative fifteenth century.

In that century,

1.   Nicholas Copernicus produced his theory that the planets in our solar system revolve around the sun,[46] which was in direct opposition to the Christian theology of the day;

2.   Henry VIII, king of England founded the Church of England which in turn set the stage for the English Reformation; and

3.   Martin Luther published The Ninety-Five Theses which marked the birth of the Protestant Church.

At the start of the fifteenth century the Catholic Church wielded absolute power in all matters. In addition to the entrenched power of its allies, the Church ruled every aspect of human life. And, as Lord Acton said four

---

46   Ptolemy of Ancient Greece had explained that the universe was a closed system revolving around the earth, and the Catholic Church concurred. During his lifetime Copernicus was afraid to publish his thesis for fear of retribution from the Catholic Church. He finally published his work in 1543, just a few weeks before he died.

centuries later, "Power tends to corrupt, and absolute power corrupts absolutely". The absolute power held by the Catholic Church resulted in flagrant abuses. Pope Sixtus IV (1471–1484), for example derived income by imposing a license on brothels and a special tax on priests who kept a mistress. He also established the practice of selling indulgences,[47] in which the Church would indulge the sins of the wealthy in return for the payment of money to shorten their time in purgatory. Pope Alexander VI (1492–1503)[48], possibly the most promiscuous of all popes, fathered seven children, including Lucrezia and Cesare Borgia[49], by at least two mistresses.

Martin Luther, a German priest and professor of theology spoke out against these abuses. He initiated the Protestant Reformation by strongly opposing the concept of indulgences and disputing the claim that freedom from God's punishment of sin could be purchased with money. Luther directly challenged the authority of the pope by teaching that the bible is the only source of divinely revealed knowledge. His refusal to retract his writings resulted in his excommunication by the pope and condemnation as an outlaw by the emperor.

In the beginning, the Protestant Reformation was simply an attempt by Western European Catholics to reform the Catholic Church. But without a central theology, the reformers soon disagreed among themselves and split according to doctrinal differences. This resulted in the establishment of different and rival Protestant Churches such as the Lutheran, the Reformed, the Calvinist, and the Presbyterian. The division of religious power among the various Protestant Churches in addition to the Catholic Church led to energetic competition and a new power alignment. By 1555 the ruler of each German state — originally empow-

---

47 According to the Catholic Church, an indulgence is a sacrifice made to reduce the time one needs to spend in purgatory after death. There are two kinds, plenary (all sins forgiven) and partial (some sins forgiven). In the middle ages bishops would sell "indulgences" to wealthy people so that the rich could live however they wanted.

48 It is interesting to note that he was pope during the expulsion of the Jews from Spain.

49 Lucrezia Borgia's family came to epitomize the ruthless Machiavellian politics and sexual corruption characteristic of the Renaissance papacy.

ered by the Holy Roman Empire — was allowed to determine the religion, Catholic or Protestant, of his own area. As a result, by 1570, barely half a century after Martin Luther posted his Ninety-Five Theses, 70% of the German population was Protestant. The power of the Holy Roman Empire diminished as the strength of the independent princes grew. With that growing independence came the first glimmers of light that marked the beginning of the enlightenment.

The rivalry and disunity of the princes grew, and without the strong central authority that was formerly exerted by the Holy Roman Empire, anarchy became the rule and small domestic wars broke out in many places. What had begun as an opportunity for greater autonomy and freedom of religion turned into major disputes over territorial, dynastic and religious issues.

Germany became a threat to itself and to the balance of power in Europe. When France and Austria joined the internal German conflict in 1618, the Thirty Years War began. It was a struggle of German Protestant princes against those loyal to the Holy Roman Empire and their dominant ruling supporters, the Hapsburgs[50]. But it soon became a general European war, fought mainly in Germany. As the battle spread throughout Germany it eventually involved many other countries on both sides. At times Sweden, Denmark, England, Netherlands, Bohemia, Bavaria and even Spain, Portugal and Italy were involved. What had begun as a war over religion quickly became one of territorial rights.

By 1635 Germany was in economic ruin but still the battles continued. The war had resulted in the death of nearly a third of the German population and unfathomable destruction. Peace negotiations were begun in 1640 but so many countries and interests were involved that battles continued until 1648 when a general settlement, the Peace of Westphalia, finally marked the end of the Thirty Years War.

The most transformational result of the war was the end of the Holy Roman Empire as an effective ruling entity, and the decline of Hapsburg

---

50   The House of Hapsburg was one of the most important royal houses of Europe and is best known for being the source of all of the formally elected Holy Roman Emperors between 1438 and 1740, as well as rulers of the Austrian and Spanish Empires.

power. This marked an important step towards religious tolerance and the beginning of the modern European state system. Although neither the Protestants nor the Catholics were completely victorious, the clear loser was the papal dreams of an empire, united under a Catholic Church.

Max Weber, a twentieth century German sociologist, economist, and politician wrote in his famous thesis *The Protestant Ethic and the Spirit of Capitalism* that the primary result of all this turmoil was that large numbers of people began developing their own enterprises and engaging in trade. The accumulation of wealth from this new trade resulted in investment in growing enterprises. In other words, the Protestant Reformation was a force behind the unplanned and uncoordinated development of capitalism, *and the eventual liberation of the Jewish psyche.*

The Age of Enlightenment, 1690s to 1805

The following analysis was adapted from material by Paul Brians, Emeritus Professor of English, Washington State University:

> Although the title "Age of Enlightenment" implies sudden discovery, what happened in the early eighteenth century might better be called the age of awakening. At its heart, the intellectual movement called "The Enlightenment" was a conflict between religion, which demanded blind faith, and reason, which sought to find natural laws in human affairs similar to the scientific laws of the physical universe.

These "humanists" argued that creative people like artists, architects, musicians, and scholars, were fulfilling divine purposes by exercising their intellectual and creative powers. They said that, by emphasizing the reasoning capacities of the human race, they were worshiping God more appropriately than the priests who harped on original sin.

The proponents of the Enlightenment believed that society would become perfect if people were free to use their reason. Human minds, they said, were designed to act rationally and would naturally seek to further the happiness of others.

Most of the Enlightenment's thinkers believed passionately in human progress through education. Michel de Montaigne, a pioneering sixteenth century French philosopher whose father had been a French Roman Catholic soldier in Italy and whose mother, Antoinette López de

Villanueva[51], was a decendant of a Spanish Jewish convert to Catholicism, asked the important question: "What do I know?" By this he meant that we must examine the world through our own eyes. He favored empirical experience over theoretical knowledge. If we cannot be certain, he argued, that our values are God-given, then we have no right to impose them by force on others. Inquisitors, popes, and kings, he argued, had no business enforcing adherence to particular religious or philosophical beliefs. This earth-shattering argument opened the door, albeit just a crack, for the revival of Judaism.

This thin trickle of thought traveled through an era otherwise dominated by dogma and fanaticism. The seventeenth century was torn by witch-hunts and wars of religion and imperial conquest. Catholics and Protestants of varying sects denounced each other as followers of Satan, and people could be punished for attending the wrong church, or for not attending any. All publications were subject to censorship both by the church and the state. The despotism of monarchs was supported by the doctrine of "divine right of kings[52]," and scripture was quoted to show that revolution was detested by God.

By the start of the eighteenth century the various Protestant sects had begun to compete with each other, producing a bewildering array of churches each claiming the exclusive path to salvation. As a result, many intellectuals began to wonder whether any of the churches or the other institutions deserved the authority they claimed.

---

51 Antoinette de Lopez de Villanueva, came from a Spanish Jewish family. One of her ancestors, Mayer Pacagon of Catalayud, was forcibly converted to Catholicism and took the name of Lopez de Villanueva. His descendants, however, remained secretly faithful to Judaism, and several of them were persecuted by the Inquisition. One of them, Juan de Villanueva, from whom Montaigne's mother was descended, fled to Toulouse, France, where he settled. She later married the Catholic Eyquem de Montaigne, her uncle's business partner.

52 The divine right of kings asserts that a monarch is subject to no earthly authority, and derives his right to rule directly from the will of God. The king is thus not subject to the will of his people, the aristocracy, or the church. According to this doctrine, since only God can judge an unjust king, if the king is in power, God must approve and any attempt to depose the king or to restrict his powers is contrary to the will of God and thus, may constitute heresy.

Absolutist kings continued to claim "divine right" and dogmatic churches continued to insist that the Church was the only source of truth and that all who lived outside its bounds were damned. But the winds of change had made their impression. Enlightened writers and speakers challenged the omnipresent censorship and sought whatever means they could to evade or even denounce it. The struggle was complex, but eventually, individualism and freedom replaced authority and tradition. Religion survived, but under the Enlightenment it was weakened and often transformed almost beyond recognition.

The Enlightenment resulted in a total social and cultural upheaval. Topics of discussion that had previously been the exclusive territory of state and religious authorities were now open to the public. As access to information increased, the demand for more information grew and a large variety of new information sharing institutions arose. The most influential of these new institutions, which will be discussed in greater detail in the coming pages, were the Academies and Learned Societies, The Republic of Letters, Coffee Houses and Cafes, Debating Societies, and Salons. The primary effect of the information sharing that occurred as a result of the development of these institutions was the great leveling of society, and the increased open participation of Jews.

Academies and Learned Societies

Prior to the eighteenth century universities were elite institutions that were generally either church related and designed to produce clergymen, or run by the local royalty to produce graduates who would serve the needs of the community in the fields of law and medicine. Some universities also offered studies in philosophy. The method used in these universities was to transmit information from the faculty to the students in as complete a fashion as possible. Students were expected to absorb the teachings so that they could serve the community in whatever discipline they had chosen. For both religious and governmental reasons, independent thought and research was discouraged.

The Academies and Learned Societies, on the other hand, were not affiliated with the universities. They were organized around new disciplines that were not being taught in the Universities. They focused on the sciences and helped promote independent research. In addition to being a fertile training ground for new scientists, these Academies and Learned Societies provided opportunities for free and open discussion among people with similar interests. The Academies and Learned Societies considered themselves institutions for *creating* knowledge, as opposed to the universities which were places for *transmitting* it.

One of the main differences between the universities and the Academies and Learned Societies was that the Learned Societies and Academies were not restricted to the privileged classes. As a result they offered an opportunity for the newly sophisticated urban entrepreneurs to satisfy their curiosity, increase their knowledge, and demonstrate their contemporary sociability. The number of Academies and Learned Societies grew exponentially after 1700, and dozens of unofficial organizations existed in addition to the formally chartered institutions.

Although they were similar in many ways, the primary difference between Learned Societies and Academies was that the Learned Societies were relatively more democratic, and the Academies, which were typical of Catholic regimes, were relatively more authoritarian.

In the late seventeenth century, L'Académie Française began to offer public contests that featured essays, poetry, and painting. The subject matter of these contests was originally religious, but by roughly 1725, in a change that was important to the emerging Jewish merchant class, the acceptable subject matter had radically expanded and diversified to include philosophical battles, and critical ruminations on the social and political institutions.

The contests were anonymous and open to all. The enforced anonymity of each submission guaranteed that neither gender, nor social rank, nor religious affiliation would affect the judging. As a result, a significant number of women participated in the competitions and although most of the contestants were from the wealthier Christian parts of society, an increasing number of Jews submitted essays, and even sometimes won.

In addition to substantial financial rewards, the contests often offered the winners the possibility of the publication of their work (often under pseudonyms). As a result, these contests stimulated a great deal of scientific and literary work which the academies and societies used to augment their research and enhance their reputation. In addition the contests animated the local, national, and international communities. The Learned Societies organized thousands of such competitions during the eighteenth and early nineteenth centuries.

Members of the academies and societies contributed to the rapid advance of the natural sciences when they presented the results of their research at society meetings. These presentations quickly became the primary vehicles for the publication of original research. Although constituting only one-quarter of contemporary journals treating the natural sciences, Learned Society[53] publications frequently contained the most original material.

Scholars and scientists often belonged to many Learned Societies at the same time. The number and quality of a person's Learned Society memberships often indicated his status in the contemporary world of learning. In some instances, full-time careers were launched as a result of membership in a scientific society.

Membership in Academies and Learned Societies, whether anonymous, under a pseudonym, or, as increasingly happened as the eighteenth century wore on, under their own name, gave Jews an opportunity to openly explore, augment and demonstrate their knowledge within the greater scientific community.

The Republic of Letters

When I was in the army, nearly half a century ago, I labored long and hard over the letters that I wrote home. There was a time period in the barracks every day in which we all, privates and officers alike, wrote our letters. Recently, after the death of my parents I came across a packet of my letters that they had kept. Upon reading them I was struck by the emotion that was conveyed in those letters, not through their content, but through the feelings buried in their carefully chosen words.

Communication in the twenty-first century has become nearly as natural as breathing. We text on our iPhones, rush to our computers to respond to email, Facebook, twitter and who knows what else. The art

---

53 The first Learned Society in the United States was founded by Benjamin Franklin in 1743 and continues today as the American Philosophical Society.

of letter writing has been all but forgotten, and with it the care that was involved. But in eighteenth century Europe, universal mail service was just being born, and the art of letter writing was indeed an art. The invention of the fountain pen was still a hundred years in the future and the typewriter was not invented until 1867. Letters were laboriously written by hand with a pen with a nib that had to be dipped into an inkwell every few words. One's penmanship was nearly as important as one's grooming and choice of clothing. As Mohini Lal Mazumdar writes in The Imperial Post Offices of British India (Calcutta, Phila Publications, 1990),

> In ancient times the kings, emperors, rulers, zamindars[54] or the feudal lords protected their land through the intelligence services of specially trained police or military agencies and courier services to convey and obtain information through runners, messengers and even through pigeons. The chief of the secret service, known as the postmaster, maintained the lines of communication ... The people used to send letters to [their] distant relatives through their friends or neighbors.

Probably, the first postal service was in Rome around the start of the Common Era. It was the first true mail service and it offered a two tier system not unlike today's US Mail. The high speed service (today's equivalent of first class mail) was provided with light carriages and fast horses. The slower service (parcel post) was equipped with two-wheeled carts pulled by oxen. Both services were restricted to government correspondence. Another service for citizens was later added.

In the United Kingdom, prior to 1840 the postal system was expensive, confusing and corrupt. Letters were paid for by the recipient rather than the sender, and were charged according to the distance the letter had traveled and the number of sheets of paper it contained. Around the middle of the nineteenth century the concept of prepayment was introduced along with adhesive postage stamps as a way to get the sender to pay for the postage. These reforms changed the face of the postal service forever.

But in eighteenth century Europe, at the start of the Enlightenment, these reforms had not yet been conceived. Most letters were delivered by messenger, and communication by means of letters was one of the

---

54 Zamindars were considered to be equivalent to lords and barons. In some cases they were also seen as independent, sovereign princes. Many zamindars were Indian princes who had lost their sovereignty due to British rule.

primary means of sharing and obtaining information. The letters were carefully and laboriously written, and they were studied and treasured by their recipients. Those members of the intellectual community in the late seventeenth and eighteenth centuries in Europe and America who communicated by mail were often referred to as the Republic of Letters.

As is evident from the name, the circulation of handwritten letters enabled intellectuals to correspond with each other across great distances, and it was a "Republic" because the letters implied a certain equality between its members. The citizens of the Republic of Letters corresponded by letter, exchanged published papers and pamphlets, and considered it their duty to bring others into the Republic through the expansion of correspondence.

The Republic of Letters was a self-proclaimed community of scholars and literary figures that stretched across national boundaries. Through communications via mail, they gathered the intellectuals of the Age of Enlightenment into a single multi-faceted communication system. The modern day reference, *men of letters* is an outgrowth of this period of communication by letters.

The Republic of Letters epitomized the ideals of the Enlightenment: an egalitarian community that was governed by knowledge and spanned political, sexual, and religious boundaries. Because it provided a forum that allowed and even encouraged "free public examination of questions regarding religion or legislation," it opened the door for Jewish intellectuals to participate in the exchange of information that was based more on intellectual integrity and less on source.

The Book Industry

As the frequency, depth, and volume of these letters increased, many of them were bound together to form scientific and literary journals. These journals offered an alternative to the established "authorities" by focusing on what was new, innovative, or challenging. They often competed to be the first to offer a new philosophical position or a new scientific discovery. In this way, they effectively promoted the new "enlightened" ideals of toleration and intellectual objectivity. By focusing on science and reason, these journals further opened the door to Jewish intellectual participation on the world stage.

The Republic of Letters was closely identified with the written word and these journals represented a new and different way of communication. The ideals of the Republic of Letters as a community, was, in this way, expressed in journals; both through their statements of purpose in prefaces and introductions, and in their actual contents. Just as the original goal of a letter had been to connect and inform two people, the goal of the journal was to inform many. In fulfilling this public role, the Republic of Letters' journals became the personification of the group as a whole.

In the beginning, the audience and authorship of these literary journals was largely the Republic of Letters itself. But soon, with the growth of the reading public, a wider audience developed, and along with this expansion came the development of periodicals.

Once the idea of periodicals was established it was only a matter of time before printers would realize that the general reading public was also interested in the world of scholarship. As readership increased, a new tone, language, and content evolved which redefined the Republic of Letters for a new audience. They separated into two schools: those who took an active role by writing and instructing others, and those who contented themselves with reading books and following the debates in the journals. The Republic of Letters, which had formerly been the exclusive domain of scientists and intellectuals, now became the province of the intellectually curious.

At the same time that the Republic of Letters was expanding its appeal, reading in general was undergoing serious changes. Until 1750 the relatively limited population of literate people tended to own a small number of books and read them repeatedly. But then, beginning in the last half of the eighteenth century and accelerating rapidly in the nineteenth century, literacy increased and people began to read as many books as they could find. State run "universal libraries" began to appear and, as demand grew, there were an increasing number of low cost books being produced. University libraries lent out their material for a small price and occasionally bookstores offered small lending libraries to their patrons. Like the journals, printed books intensified and multiplied the circulation of information. And Jews, with their high literacy rate were important beneficiaries of this expansion.

This increased consumption of reading materials was one of the key features of the Enlightenment. Growing demand and the refinement of the printing press[55] allowed publishers to offer printed materials in greater quantities at lower prices which further encouraged the spread of books, pamphlets, newspapers and journals. For the first time, the reading public extended beyond the realm of the upper classes.

Of course, censorship was rampant and European booksellers and publishers had to negotiate censorship laws of varying strictness. Often, books were condemned by the royalty and/or the Church. But the publishers and booksellers found ways to circumvent the harsh censorship and a healthy, and mostly legal, publishing industry developed throughout Europe.

Coffee Houses and Cafes

In the United States, the French word for coffeehouse (café) implies an informal restaurant, offering a range of hot meals, but in Europe, where it originated, a café or coffee house was an establishment which primarily served coffee or other hot beverages. It was a unique amalgamation of a bar and a restaurant. From a cultural standpoint, coffeehouses largely served as centers of social interaction: the coffeehouse provided social members with a place to congregate, talk, write, read, and entertain one another, either individually or in small groups of two or three.

Europeans first learned about coffee through reports brought back by travelers from the Ottoman Empire who reported how men would consume an intoxicating liquor, "black in color and made by infusing the powdered berry of a plant that flourished in Arabia". Native men, they said, consumed this liquid "all day long and far into the night, with no apparent desire for sleep but with mind and body continuously alert, [these] men talked and argued, finding in the hot black liquor a curious stimulus quite unlike that produced by fermented juice of grape."

---

55 The rotary printing press was invented in 1819 but it is the cylinder press, which was invented in 1846 that could print 8,000 sheets an hour, that marks the start of newspapers.

Although coffee had been known in France since the 1640s, and the first café had been established in Paris in 1686, it took coffee a while to become popular. But by the 1720s there were around 400 cafés in the city.

Some of these coffee houses presented an opportunity for free and far ranging conversation. Like-minded scholars congregated to read, learn from and debate with each other. Unlike the formal universities and governmental institutions, or the Academies and Learned Societies, conversation in the coffee houses was freer and far ranging. These so called penny universities occupied a significant position in academic life because they offered an opportunity for wide ranging discussions that could not be conducted under more formal circumstances.

The coffee houses were great social levelers, open to all men (the banning of women from coffee houses, though not universal, appears to have been common in Europe) regardless of social status. As a result they were philosophical sources of equality and republicanism and they offered a neutral location for the emerging Jewish intellectuals to share their insights and enthusiasms. In the more general population, coffee houses often functioned as meeting places where business could be carried on, news exchanged and government policies discussed. Each of the Coffeehouses attracted a particular clientele that was characterized by occupation or attitude, such as merchants, lawyers, booksellers, authors, and various men of fashion.

By espousing experimental and innovative philosophies in art, culture, and politics, the coffee houses pushed against the boundaries of what had previously been accepted as the norm or the status quo. Essentially, they integrated the elite libraries, schools and colleges into the public sphere. In the liberal and flexible atmosphere of the coffee houses, discussions often ranged from experimental philosophy to contemporary politics and religion, and the new sciences, as well as the newly emerging literature and fashions.

By the middle of the 18th century, every major city in Europe boasted at least one coffee house, if not several, and these not only affected European drinking habits, but also ushered in new forms of social life. In the coffee house, mental and intellectual alertness set the tone rather than intoxication and abandonment. As havens of sobriety, coffee houses soon became favorite meeting-places and focal points of communication for the new upwardly-mobile middle class. It was in coffee houses that the latest news and gossip was passed on. They became, in effect, "information exchanges", where numerous foreign newspapers were available and where business relationships could be forged. Throughout Europe, coffee houses soon became focal points of the Enlightenment and of political activity.

Coffee houses largely remained a male preserve up to the middle of the nineteenth century. The rational, shrewd, outward-looking and politically active man was expected to involve himself in the tough, competitive world of commerce, while the woman's sphere of activity was the home and the family. Accordingly, women were excluded from the bourgeois public realm, from the world of politics and consequently, from the coffee houses. However, all that would change with the advent of salons.

Salons

Prior to the mid eighteenth century most parents outside of the nobility saw no benefit in educating their daughters. But the women of the newly affluent middle class, who had been denied a proper education, were eager to achieve the intellectual sophistication of the upper classes. These socially and intellectually ambitious women sought to satisfy their urgent need for education by associating with modern day intellectuals. For these women, the salon was a socially acceptable substitute for the formal education that had been denied to them. Thus, invitations to these ladies' salons were not based on social standing or religious affiliation, but rather on a person's intelligence, wit and conversation. And, being attractive or somewhat controversial was always an added bonus.

Salons were usually held in the home of an inspiring hostess and were a gathering place for the intellectual, social, political, and cultural elites. These real and aspiring elites came partly to amuse one another and partly to refine their taste and increase their knowledge through conversation.

Although salons had originated among the intellectually ambitious women of the emerging middle class, many ladies of the aristocracy began hosting small gatherings in their townhouses in Paris as well. The court at Versailles, which had previously been the locale of stimulating conversation, had become a dull and stuffy environment where titles and social status meant everything and the smallest faux pas was tantamount to social death. As a result the elite sought a place where they could freely laugh and be merry without upsetting the rigidly controlled French court. People from the most esteemed parts of society came together in these salons for an evening of debate and conversation. Enlightened thinkers, aristocrats, high ranking military officers and exotic foreigners mingled together on equal footing.

These salons enabled nobility, artists and thinkers to exchange ideas across barriers of class, gender, nationality, economic standing, and religion; even though society was still rigidly defined along these lines. And women and Jews — especially Jewish women, whose participation in official public life was restricted by various barriers — played a prominent role. At a time when society was defined and regulated by Christian men; women and Jews now had the opportunity to be a powerful influence. In the salon, where the hostesses carefully selected their guests, chose the subjects of their meetings, and when necessary, directed the discussion, intellectual fluency and achievement was often more highly valued than religion, affluence, position or title.

The salon was thus an informal university for women in which they were able to exchange ideas, receive and give criticism, read and perform their own works and hear the works and ideas of others. By the end of the century, these salons had become quite common among the elite as well as the newly emerging middle class.

The salons were also a place in which the merchants could obtain and exchange information about distant markets as well as debate matters like the growth of democracy and individual liberty. These face-to-face meetings served as a counterweight to political authority.

Starting in the 1830s, with the rise of the middle and merchant classes a new hierarchy of social, cultural, political, and philosophical attitudes took shape. This class derived its social and economic power from erudition, employment, education, and wealth, as distinguished from the social classes whose inherited power came from being born into an aristocratic family of titled land owners.

Increasingly, affluent Jews sought to immerse themselves in Europe's rich cultural life. But they had to learn to recognize the opportunities and pitfalls of the new social order without the comfort and support of a secure community. For Jewish women, their ambitions to enter the upper echelons of society faced the double obstacles of continuing anti-Semitism and deeply entrenched gender role restrictions. Thus, from 1800 on, the salons performed a political and social miracle. The Jewish women's newly acquired education, affluence, and sophistication enabled them to establish a venue in their homes in which Jews and non-Jews, men and women, could meet in relative equality. Like-minded people could study art, literature, philosophy or music together. Through this intellectual emancipation, cultured Jewish women were able to escape the restrictions of their social ghetto. In these mixed gatherings of nobles, high civil servants, writers, philosophers, artists and musicians, these Jewish women created a radical vehicle for democratization, in which patrons and artists had the opportunity to freely exchange ideas.

Among the first Jewish salonières were Henriette Herz and Rahel Levin Varnhagen in 1780s Berlin; Fanny von Arnstein and her sister Cäcilie von Eskeles in Vienna; then there were the famed music salons of Amalie Beer and Fanny Mendelssohn Hensel (the sister of Felix) in Berlin; the 1890s literary salons of Ada Leverson in London and Geneviève Straus in Paris; the subversive political salon of Anna Kuliscioff in Milan; and the modernist art salons of Berta Szeps Zuckerkandl in Vienna and Margherita Sarfatti in Milan.

Debating Societies

The world was awakening as if from a deep sleep. The oppressive restrictions of the Catholic Church had been lifted, and the Holy Roman Empire, with its puppet monarchies had been shaken to its foundation. The Protestant Reformation and the Industrial Revolution had begun shifting the balance of power away from the landed aristocracy toward the new middle class. By the time of the second wave of the Industrial Revolution in the late eighteen hundreds with its introduction of steam-powered ships, railways, the internal combustion engine and electrical power generation, the new middle class, and the growing banking class had assumed power. The thirst for knowledge on every level became the central motivating force. Whereas most of the art and culture had previously been the private domain of the aristocracy, new museums, libraries and concert halls appeared which opened the world of culture and learning to the middle class. And along with this tidal wave of change, the Jews who were in many ways a central force of the emerging middle class, sought to reach cultural levels that previously had only been available to the nobility or the church.

Self improvement was the order of the day, and the debating clubs provided an opportunity for socialization, entertainment, and self improvement. At first, these self improvement groups took the form of literary or reading societies, similar in many ways to today's book clubs. Many of these societies debated topical issues, with members designated to present cases for and against. These organizations met regularly, usually through the winter months. Some subscribed to monthly journals, others were attached to libraries and some even started their own libraries.

The usual format for these literary societies was that members would present analyses of chosen works to the assembled society, which would then discuss and debate them. As these reading groups grew they evolved into debating clubs whose purpose was "the moral and intellectual improvement of the members and the promotion of social intercourse between them". These clubs often affiliated with similar organizations, and went on outings to sites of interest, and presented dramatic entertainment. One of the primary advantages of membership in these debating societies was the formation of friendships and alliances outside of one's comfort zone.

Some of these societies encouraged members to write poetry and articles that were read (anonymously) aloud to the other members, who then gave their opinion. The debating societies discussed an extremely wide range of topics of which a common theme was often women. Societies debated over "male and female qualities," courtship, marriage, and the role of women in the public sphere. The societies also discussed political issues, current events, and religion. But the subject matter of these debates did not usually translate into action.

From a historical standpoint, one of the most important features of the debating societies was their openness to the public. They were open to all classes providing they could pay the usually modest entrance fee. Some debating clubs became quite large-scale businesses that charged admission fees and were often highly successful commercial enterprises. Some of the larger societies welcomed from 800 to 1200 spectators a night. Once inside, spectators were able to participate in a largely egalitarian form of sociability.

Debating societies offered: "the appeal and purposes of meetings that combined instruction with entertainment, gentility with mass audiences, and affairs of state with affairs of the heart." Debating societies would rent a hall, charge an admission, and allow the public to discuss a wide variety of topics in the public sphere. What separated them from other institutions is that they specifically invited women to partake in their discussions. Unlike the salons, women were there to participate as equals, not as hosts. And, since some of these debates occasionally ended in violence, the restraining presence of women was especially welcome

Dawn in the Diaspora

For nearly two thousand years the unaffiliated Jews lived in a "no mans land." Since they had chosen not to live within the confines of the "traditional" rabbinic Jewish community and they could not live freely in the gentile community, they were, as in the poem "The Lay of the Last Minstrel" by Sir Walter Scott cited in the beginning of this book, men without a country. They were constantly mobile — doing whatever they had to do to survive in a hostile world environment, while maintaining their public anonymity as well as their private Jewish identity.

They educated their children as well as they could and they equipped them with the necessary social and intellectual survival skills. Herbert Spencer's phrase "survival of the fittest" clearly applied to these unaffiliated Jewish survivors. They were tough, and wily, and socially aware. They recognized threats and opportunities long before they became apparent to the general population, and they adapted more easily to change; and only the fittest survived as Jews.

Although their Jewish identity was affirmed through the observance of private Jewish rituals, their public identity was circumspect at best.

The greatest institutional threat to their survival came from the Catholic Church; its leaders, officials and acolytes.

In the sixteen hundreds the Protestant reformation weakened the hold that the Holy Roman Empire had had on free expression. By the eighteenth century, although the influence of the Catholic Church had sharply diminished, the royal court and the landed nobility were still the centers of high culture. The opulence of their magnificent buildings, ornate tapestries, exquisite collections of paintings and lavish soirees, assured them of social and cultural domination. But by the end of the century high culture started to move out of the narrow confines of the court and into coffee houses, reading societies, debating clubs, assembly rooms, galleries and concert halls. "Culture" had become an active partner of commerce and was no longer the exclusive province of royalty and clergy. As a result a more secular tone was established throughout Europe.

Personal realization and achievement began to outweigh family and birth-status and the exchange of ideas was encouraged, not for their source, but for their originality. Truth was a very real thing that was accessible to those with the discipline and energy to seek it; and truth was inseparable from human experience and interaction. Truth, according to the new intellectual society, was incompatible with historic social, religious and sexual prejudices.

And the wandering Jews who had lived for so many centuries in anonymity, were among the primary beneficiaries of this new openness. Two distinct groups of Jews emerged: those who were willing to abandon their ties to traditional Judaism in order to achieve social status; and those who sought to adapt Judaism to the new realities of the nineteenth century. The intellectual and commercial world was enticing them out of the secure shadows in which they had survived for so many generations, but how far could they stretch the bonds that tied them to Judaism before they broke?

THE EVOLVING POLITICAL ENVIRONMENT: THE JEWISH POPULATION CENTERS OF THE DIASPORA

Three Jewish population centers evolved after the destruction of the second Temple and the subsequent Diaspora. With the growing influence of Christianity, the atmosphere in the Roman Empire became increasingly hostile toward Jews and two new migrations from Rome developed: One to the east across the Adriatic Sea to Lithuania, Belarus, Ukraine and Russia and along the shores of the Black Sea, and the other to the west, along the coast of the Mediterranean to Spain. Chronologically, the first, and longest lasting Jewish population center was in Russia which lasted, without interruption, from before the destruction of the Second Temple to today. The second, and arguably the greatest, was in Spain and lasted five hundred years, from the eighth century to the fifteenth century. The third was in Poland and lasted for four hundred years from the sixteenth century to the twentieth century. As we will see in the coming sections, the Jews in Poland and Spain, at the height of their residency, lived in relative safety and comfort. In Russia, although there were occasional localized pogroms, and peasant rampages, the Jews, for the most part, were an integral and essential part of Russian society[56].

Spain

From the second half of the eighth century to the end of the eleventh century Jewish life in Spain flourished. Jews made major contributions in the fields of mathematics, medicine, botany, geography, poetry, philosophy, and medicine. They adopted many customs and traditions of the Moors and interweaved them into their daily life. Muslim influence on the Jews was significant in both substance and style. Ceremoniously washing of the hands and feet, upon leaving a cemetery or before entering a Synagogue, which is an Islamic custom, became adopted by Jews, and much of today's synagogue architecture and liturgical music can be traced to Moorish origins.

In the eleventh century the Iberian (Spanish) Caliphate began to disintegrate as the result of civil war, and Spain was increasingly divided into various competing Moorish Kingdoms. The armies of Christendom

---

56 Some typically Russian names like Lev might have Jewish origins.

gained a foothold on the Iberian Peninsula and life for the Jews became more difficult. Some of the Jewish population chose to leave Spain, but, even though murders and official oppression became more common, many influential Jews chose to remain. They continued their way of life under the subsequent Christian monarchs of Spain until three hundred years later, when they were expelled. The only Jews who remained were crypto-Jews called Marranos who professed conversion to Christianity but practiced their religion in secret. Many of these Marranos eventually converted to Christianity, but others maintained their secret Judaism and practiced strict endogamy[57].

Most of the Spanish Jewish exiles migrated east seeking refuge among the Slavs and the Turks in the Ottoman Empire. Some went to Holland which had invited the Jewish refugees to settle there. By the middle of the fifteenth century the Spanish Jewish population, which had been above half a million, had dropped to under 200,000, and in 1492 more than 150,000, nearly all the remaining Spanish Jews, fled the Inquisition.

These fleeing Sephardic[58] Jews settled throughout the Ottoman Empire in the southern European provinces and in the Mediterranean coastal regions. The Jewish population of Jerusalem, for example, increased from 70 families in 1488 to 1,500 at the beginning of the 16th century, and that of Safed increased from 300 to 2,000 families and almost surpassed Jerusalem in importance. Damascus had 500 Sephardic families. Istanbul had a Jewish community of 30,000 individuals with 44 synagogues. Today, nearly a thousand years later, the influence of these Sephardic Jews remains obvious to even the most casual observer. Many of the synagogues that were established remain, as well as the music and ritual. The Sephardic influence is most apparent in Israel, where Sephardic Hebrew is the spoken language. Ladino, the common language that was originally shared by Spanish Jews, remains a vibrant part of twenty-first century Jewish life.

Although their influence has survived to this day, the Diaspora communities in Spain ceased to exist after 1492 and have never revived.

---

57 Endogamy is the practice of marrying within a specific ethnic group.
58 Sephardic is the name for Jews from Spain.

Poland

The independent country of Poland, on the eastern edge of the Holy Roman Empire, was the gateway to Western Europe. It was adjacent to the countries of Bohmen (Czechoslovakia) Schlesien (Silesia) and Mahren (Moravia) which were, according to an early sixteenth century map, "Kreisfrei[59]." Hungary was part of the Ottoman Empire. Poland was independent.

We have become accustomed to "Polish jokes" that deride and stereotype Poland and its Jews. But the greatness that Poland achieved and the sad story of its decline in the eighteenth century have no equal anywhere in world history. In the seventeenth century Poland stood tall and unique among the countries of Europe. Poland was the only country in which the kings were elected from among the nobility, the only country where religious tolerance was an untouchable right. Poland was also the birthplace of public education. It is therefore not surprising that there were about 500,000 Jews[60], fully half of the known world Jewish population living in Poland in the mid seventeenth century. Five percent of the entire Polish population was Jewish. By the mid eighteenth century; sixty percent[61] of the world's known Jewish population lived in Poland because it was the most hospitable and liberal country in Europe.

Sadly, Poland was erased from the map in 1795.

Back in the sixteenth century, Poland had consisted of a number of small communities that were held together by the strong hand of Poland's dynastic monarchy. But, in 1572, following the childless death of the last king, Poland was in danger of shattering into small ethnic and religious duchies. Poland's various communities had historically been separated according to their ethnic backgrounds (Poles, Lithuanians, Slavs, Germans, Armenians, Moldavians) and their different religions (Catholic, Protestant, Eastern Orthodox, Jewish[62], and Muslim). In a remarkable historic effort to avoid civil war and strengthen the unity of the country, Polish and Lithuanian nobles gathered in Warsaw to formulate

---

59 Not part of the Holy Roman Empire
60 These are officially counted Jews. There were probably many times that number who were not counted.
61 Some estimates place this as high as 80%.
62 In mid 17th century there were an estimated 173 Jewish communities.

the Confederation of Warsaw. This Confederation unified the country by creating a new highly inclusive political system that brought all of the disparate divisions into the government. Polish kings were elected. Unlike the other European monarchs, their position was very weak because most of the powers of government were in the hands of the upper class nobility. No major law could be changed without the approval of the nobility, and some legal changes required a unanimous vote. Members of the Polish nobility were permitted to form their own militias and to engage, if necessary, in armed rebellion against the king if they thought that the agreed upon law was being broken.

The declaration of equality and religious tolerance by the Confederation was an important confirmation that the various communities stood together. This unanimity was not imposed by the government, nor was it a consequence of war; but rather, it resulted from the peaceful and unifying actions of the members of Polish-Lithuanian society.

Since this was a secular agreement, it was opposed by most of the Catholic priests and the hierarchy of the Roman Catholic Church. The only bishop that signed the protocols claimed that he did so under the "threat of the sword". Another bishop was excommunicated for signing a later similar proclamation.

For over two hundred years Poland was the most liberal country in Europe. While much of the energy of the nascent Western Enlightenment was committed to the struggle for freedom from oppressive absolute monarchies, the Polish Enlightenment was wrestling with problems that had resulted from too much freedom. And, whereas the emerging middle class was the driving force in the Western European Enlightenment movement, most of the reforms in Poland originated with the upper class nobility.

During this time Poland had no *official* religion. Although the Roman Catholic Church controlled much of the power and wealth, the Orthodox Church had more adherents. There was also a large population of Jews and Protestants. Polish nobility considered the idea of religious equality to be one of the foundations of its culture[63], and reformers fought

---

63 This is obviously the reason that there was such a large Jewish presence in Poland.

to expand it towards other social classes. Other reforms, like the creation of the world's first ministry of education, attempted to transform Poland into a modern constitutional monarchy.

But sadly, toward the end of the 18th century the nobles' democracy gradually declined into anarchy, making the once powerful Common-wealth of Poland vulnerable to foreign intervention. Eventually the coun-try was conquered and partitioned by its neighbors Russia, Prussia, and Austria and was completely erased from the map in 1795.

The Polish Jewish Community

The tandem expulsions of Jews from France in 1306 and from Ger-many in 1349 had brought many Jewish refugees to Poland from the west. These refugees merged with a different sort of Jewish population that was entering Poland from the east: The Jews of Lithuania, Belarus, Ukraine and Russia, some of whom may have lived there since the exile following the destruction of the First Temple in Jerusalem in 586 B.C.E. Also living among these Eastern European/Russian Jews was a relatively large population[64] of Karaites, who were, according to some scholars, the descendants of the Sadducees.[65]

Like the Sadducees, the Karaites followed the Hebrew Bible to the exclusion of rabbinical traditions and laws. In their declared opposition to rabbinical oral law (Halacha), the Karaite leaders proclaimed that the unrestricted study of the Bible was the only source of religion. This philosophy was especially attractive to the members of the anti-rabbinic sects, and the unaffiliated wandering Jews.

The Russian Karaites had been living in the area surrounding the Black Sea since at least the eighth century[66]. As the political atmosphere for Jews in Russia improved, the Karaites migrated to Ukraine, Belarus, Lithuania, and Poland. These Eastern European/Russian Jews were not exiles and rather than running *from* oppression, they entered Poland seeking new opportunities.

---

64 There were more than 10,000, according to some estimates.
65 The Sadducees were a first-century Jewish sect that followed the Hebrew Bible literally and rejected the Pharisees' notion of an oral Torah.
66 There is some evidence that exiles from rabbinic Judaism (the forerunners of the Karaites) had arrived in the area in the first centuries of the Common Era.

According to the Jewish Encyclopedia,

The origin of the Lithuanian Jews has been the subject of much specu-
lation. It is now almost certain that they were made up of two distinct
streams of Jewish immigration. The older of the two entered Lithuania by
way of South Russia, where Jews had lived in considerable numbers since
the beginning of the Common Era. The fact that these had adopted the
Russian language and the customs, occupations, and even the names of
the native population, serves to prove that they came from the East rather
than from Western Europe.

Armenian and Georgian historians record that after the destruction of the
First Temple (587 B.C.E.) Nebuchadnezzar deported numbers of Jewish
captives to Armenia and to the Caucasus. These exiles were joined later
by coreligionists from Media and Judea. At the end of the fourth century
there were Armenian cities possessing Jewish populations ranging from
10,000 to 30,000.

Jews had lived in Georgia also since the destruction of the First Temple.
After the capture of Jerusalem by Vespasian (70 C.E.) other Jewish exiles
joined their coreligionists at Mzchet.

Monuments consisting of marble slabs bearing Greek inscriptions show
that Jews lived in the Crimea and along the entire eastern coast of the
Black Sea at the beginning of the Common Era, and that they possessed
well-organized communities.

Jews from the Crimea moved eastward and northward and became the
founders of Jewish communities along the shores of the Caspian Sea and
of the lower Volga, carrying with them a civilization more advanced than
that of the native tribes among which they settled. It appears that the local Jewish community possessed very considerable influence. In 1321, Kiev,
Volhynia, and Podolia were conquered by the Lithuanian grand duke
Gedimin, who granted the Jewish inhabitants of these territories the same
rights that were enjoyed by his Jewish subjects in Lithuania. These rights
were subsequently amplified by the well-known charter of Witold in 1388,
under which the Jews of Kiev and of other Russian principalities were
accorded full citizenship, not a few of them serving in the body-guards of
the Russian princes.

It has been assumed that many, if not most of the Jews in Poland
were descended from refugees fleeing from the Spanish Inquisition. But
recent demographic and linguistic research indicates that since the Jews
of Poland spoke Yiddish, it is not likely that they had originated in Spain
where Ladino, an amalgam of Spanish and Hebrew, was the common
Jewish language.

The unique character, etymology and history of Yiddish have become an undecipherable riddle. George Johnson, writing in The New York Times on October 29, 1996, describes the cloudy history of the Yiddish speaking Polish Jews and illustrates the difficulty of determining their origins and composition:

> Trying to trace the ancient roots of a modern language is always a maddeningly ambiguous and uncertain enterprise. With Yiddish, the language of the Ashkenazic Jews of Central and Eastern Europe, the task is even harder because of the horrifying fact that most of the speakers were exterminated in the Holocaust.
>
> As a result, the study of Yiddish origins — and especially the touchy issue of its relationship to German — has sometimes been criticized as one in which rational analysis has been overwhelmed by emotion. But a number of recent studies are now being welcomed by linguists as evidence that the field is turning into a solid science.

These studies, according to Johnson, attempt to reconstruct the original Yiddish. In this way, the linguists hope to explain the origins of this multi faceted language which mixes Germanic grammar and vocabulary with Hebrew and Aramaic, plus a sprinkling of Slavic and ancient Romance languages.

They are hoping to determine whether, as is widely believed, Yiddish began in Western Europe and spread eastward, or whether, as an increasing number of scholars now believe, its origins were in the east and it spread westward. One linguist, Johnson points out, has recently argued that Yiddish began as a Slavic language that was "relexified," with most of its vocabulary replaced by German words but with much of its Slavic structure remaining.

Perhaps the key to these questions, according to Johnson, is the central mystery of where the Jews of Eastern Europe came from. And (in agreement with the central thesis of this book) Johnson points out that "many historians believe that there were not nearly enough Jews in Western Europe to account for the huge population that later flourished in Poland, Lithuania, Ukraine and nearby areas."

He writes that,

> Even more troublesome are demographic studies indicating that during the Middle Ages there were no more than 25,000 to 35,000 Jews in Western Europe. These figures are hard to reconcile with other studies show-

ing that by the 17th century there were hundreds of thousands of Jews in Eastern Europe.

In a paper published in 1992, Dr. Robert D. King, who holds the Audre and Bernard Rapoport Chair of Jewish Studies at the University of Texas at Austin wrote, "You just can't get those numbers by natural population increase." He suggested that the origins of Yiddish were not in the Rhineland at all, but eastward along the Danube — in Bavaria and as far east as Hungary and the Czech and Slovak lands. From there, Dr. King contends, the language radiated both westward, into the Rhineland, and eastward into Poland, Lithuania, Latvia and other areas.

By determining the sources of the Yiddish mother tongue, linguists hope to trace the migration of the Eastern European Jews and their language. Some linguists have even suggested, on the basis of linguistic evidence, that the Jews of Eastern Europe were not from the Middle East at all, but were members of another ethnic group that adopted Judaism.

Dr. King concedes that it is still possible for there to be a western origin for Yiddish: Jews that had migrated from the Rhineland may have lived in the Danube region long enough for their language to adopt local vocabulary, but he is skeptical that so much of the Rhineland German could have been so completely erased.

In agreement with the thesis of this book and contrary to the commonly held belief, Dr. King postulates that there must have already been a large population of Jews in Eastern Europe who had lived there since biblical times, coming up from the Middle East as traders speaking Hebrew and Aramaic. The Yiddish language and culture of the Danube region then diffused eastward, he says, influencing this existing population.

In an effort to reconcile the disparate views about the origins of Yiddish, Johnson concludes,

> Historians scarcely noticed these early pioneers, Dr. King speculates, because they did not have the leisure to develop the strong scholarly tradition that existed farther west. "The legacy of pre-Crusade Jewish life in Western Europe was a tradition of learning, of the rabbinate, of the community," Dr. King said. "The legacy of early Jewish life in the Slavic East was very largely the bones of its dead."

By January of 1573 when the Polish and Lithuanian nobles met at the "Conference of Warsaw" to guarantee religious rights, there already was a substantial Jewish population in Poland. As a result of this "Conference of Warsaw" Jews from Western Europe and areas as diverse as Romania, Ukraine, Belarus, Latvia, Lithuania, and even as far as Russia itself (as far east as the Urals) flocked westward to Poland[67].

There was a feeling within segments of the Jewish community that efforts should be made to integrate the Jews into the new Polish society. This action was supported by progressive Jews who were advocates of the Haskalah, and who encouraged the reform of Jewish life and the modernization of Jewish institutions and customs. In the writings of Polish liberals and Jewish integrationists of this period, there is the common assumption that Jews suffer because they persist in their separateness and that if they become more like Poles, both they and Poland[68] will prosper.

During the nineteenth century, the Jews of Poland experienced enormous demographic and economic growth. The Jewish population increased at a substantially greater rate than that of non-Jews, and Jews moved rapidly up the economic scale.

In 1816 Jews constituted 8.7% of the population. By 1865, just fifty years later, that number had grown to 13.5% *of the total Polish population.* By the end of the century, despite the large-scale Polish-Jewish emigration to the United States, 14% of Poland's citizens were Jews. This increase was accompanied by the rapid urbanization of Polish Jewry. In 1856 nearly one third of Poland's Jewish population lived in Warsaw.

Increasingly, the Jews of Poland in the 19th century lived primarily in cities. In 1827, 80% of Polish Jews lived in cities and by 1865 that percentage had increased to over 91%. This means that fewer than 10% of

---

67 In 1795, Poland ceased to exist as a political entity, and the country was partitioned, the Jews of Poland became subjects of Russia, Austria, and Prussia.

68 The geographic entity "Poland" from this point forward refers to that area of the Polish commonwealth which, by 1795, had been divided between Austria and Prussia and which subsequently constituted the basis of the grand duchy of Warsaw, created in 1807. Following the Congress of Vienna in 1815 much of this area was annexed to the Russian Empire as the semi-autonomous Kingdom of Poland, also known as Congress Poland. The kingdom constituted the core of ethnic Poland, the center of Polish politics and culture, and an economic area of great importance. It does not include Austrian Poland (Galicia), Prussian Poland (Poznan, Silesia, and Pomerania), and the Russian northwestern region also known as Lithuania-Belorussia.

Poland's Jews lived in "shtetles". This is far different from the commonly held ("Fiddler on the Roof") misconception of Polish Jewish history.

While Jews had historically predominated in trade, their growth and influence during the 19th century was remarkable. In 1815, for example, 1,657 Polish Jews participated at the Leipzig trade fair compared with 143 Polish gentiles. During the course of the century, as the Jews increasingly dominated the cities, their role in urban commercial ventures became more pronounced. In fact, in 1862 nearly 90% of Warsaw's shopkeepers were Jewish.

A wealthy Jewish merchant and financial class emerged that played a historically important role in the urbanization and industrialization of Poland. There were thousands of independent Jewish artisans (some 119,000, according to the survey of the Jewish Colonization Association (ICA) in 1898) who worked in tiny shops with rarely more than one employee. Even in major cities like Lodz and Bialystok the typical Jewish weaver was a private entrepreneur who worked in a small shop or at home, not in a large factory.

By the end of the century, eighteen out of twenty six major private banks in Warsaw were owned by Jews or Jewish converts to Christianity. This highly influential Jewish professional class was active in both Jewish and non-Jewish political and cultural movements. It also provided important new leadership for the Jewish community. This was part of a "Polish orientation" among Jews who believed that Polish independence would also lead to the disappearance of anti-Semitism. *Izraelita*,[69] the Polish-Jewish periodical advocating integration, began publication in 1866, and a number of Jewish intellectuals hoped for the eventual total integration of the Jews into the Polish nation.

The Polish Enlightenment

The Polish Enlightenment, which occurred somewhat earlier than the enlightenment in the rest of Europe, differed from them in one important aspect. The Western Enlightenment originated with the bourgeoisie

---

69 *The Israelita* was a Jewish weekly in the Polish language, published in Warsaw since 1865, that was strongly opposed by Orthodox Jews. The *Izraelita* advised the Orthodox Jews to introduce the Polish language in the heder and it urged the Liberals to teach their children Hebrew.

who had been dominated by the aristocracy and was starved for equality; while the Polish Enlightenment originated with the Polish aristocracy who encouraged and nurtured the Polish bourgeoisie.

In the second half of the eighteenth century the ideas that had been developed as a result of the Polish Enlightenment had a significant impact abroad. Polish writers produced a large quantity of political, primarily constitutional, writing which emphasized the constitutional differences between Poland and other European countries.

As a result of the partitions in 1795, Poles were forced to seek a new life in Europe. Polish poets, politicians, noblemen, writers, and artists became the European, and American revolutionaries of the nineteenth century. Their history of, and desire for freedom and liberty became one of the defining characteristics of Polish émigrés. Polish revolutionaries[70] participated in uprisings in Prussia, the Austrian Empire, Imperial Russia, and the United States. Polish legions fought alongside Napoleon and participated in the Hungarian Revolution in 1848.

Poland was briefly resurrected as a smaller country in 1807 when Napoleon set up the Duchy of Warsaw. But after his defeat and the implementation of the Congress of Vienna treaty in 1815, Russia gained the largest share of Poland, including Warsaw. Under Russian rule, Poles faced confiscation of property, deportation, forced military service, and the closure of their once proud universities. In 1863 the Poles revolted against the harsh Russian rule. The uprising began as a spontaneous protest by young Poles against conscription into the Russian Army, and was soon joined by high-ranking Lithuanian officers and various politicians.

---

70 Perhaps the best known of these revolutionaries was Thaddeus Kosciusko (1746–1817), who fought in the American Revolution. He studied military engineering in Paris and went to America in 1776, where he joined the colonial army. He helped build fortifications in Philadelphia, Pa., and at West Point, N.Y. As chief of engineers, he twice rescued the army of Gen. Nathanael Greene by directing river crossings. He also directed the blockade of Charleston, S.C. At the war's end he was awarded U.S. citizenship and made a brigadier general. He returned to Poland in 1784 and became a major general in the Polish army. In 1794 he led a rebellion against occupying Russian and Prussian forces, during which he defended Warsaw for two months, directing residents to build earthworks. He was jailed in Russia from 1794 to 1796, returned to the U.S. in 1797, and then left for France, where he continued efforts to secure Polish independence.

But the insurrectionists, who were severely outnumbered and lacked serious outside support, were forced to resort to guerrilla warfare tactics. They failed to win any major military victories or capture any major cities or fortresses in Russian-occupied lands.

Severe reprisals against the insurgents, such as public executions and deportations to Siberia, led many Poles to abandon the armed struggle. They turned, instead to the goal of achieving economic and cultural self-improvement, but Russification of Polish secondary schools was imposed and the literacy rate dropped dramatically.

In the Austrian portion, Poles fared better, and were allowed to have representation in Parliament and to form their own universities. Kraków and Lemberg (Lwów/Lviv) became centers of Polish culture and education.

In the Prussian (German) section Prussia Germanized the entire school system and showed no more respect for Polish culture and institutions than had the Russian Empire.

As is often the case, while much of Europe condemned the dismemberment of Poland as an international crime without historical parallel, no state actively opposed the annexations

The rabbinic Jews of Europe, who had flocked to Poland seeking freedom and equal rights and had established large workable communities, now became the subjects of the various conquering countries. The freedoms which they had once sought, and for the most part achieved, had been taken away, and their once thriving communities now drifted into poverty and isolation[71].

Russia

Unlike sophisticated Poland, Russia was a powerful yet totally primitive empire. Peter the Great, who assumed full Tsarist power in 1696 and reigned until 1725, had traveled extensively throughout Europe and was greatly influenced by the ideas of style and commerce that were beginning to appear in Western Europe. On his assumption of power he introduced Western-type clothing, factories, and schools in Russia. He reor-

---

71 Much of the "traditional" clothing worn by today's ultra orthodox sects is an effort to resurrect the grandeur that had been achieved in the Polish rabbinic communities of the 18th century

ganized Russia's government to make it run more efficiently and forced Russia's nobility to adopt many Western customs. He also increased the czar's power over the aristocrats, church officials, and serfs.

Peter promoted the arts and many new schools were started, mainly for the upper classes. The Russian Imperial School of Ballet was founded, and Italian opera and chamber music were performed for the first time in Russia. It also became fashionable in Russia to espouse the newest Western ideas on freedom and social reform, although these "liberal" attitudes did not filter down to the vast peasant class.

In 1742 Elizabeth Petrovna, the illegitimate daughter of Peter the Great, assumed the throne. Also known as Elizabeth I, she reigned from 1742 to 1761.

She was a passionate church attendee and was especially harsh in enforcing anti-Jewish legislation. In her edict expelling the Jews from Little Russia (now called Ukraine) she stated that "no other fruit may be expected from the haters of Christ the Savior's name than extreme injury to our faithful subjects." When the merchants of Riga, the capital of Latvia and financial center of the Baltic's territories (Latvia, Lithuania, and Estonia) advised the empress that a more liberal treatment of the Jews would benefit the imperial treasury, Elizabeth wrote on the margin of the report: "I will not derive any profit from the enemies of Christ."

On December 25, 1761, Elizabeth died leaving the throne to her nephew, Peter II who died shortly thereafter. His wife, Sophia of Zerbst, who would later be called Catherine the Great, (1762–1796) succeeded him.

Catherine the Great, one of Russia's greatest leaders in the tsarist period, recognized the importance of the Jewish merchants to the commercial growth of the empire, and so she encouraged an easing of the existing laws:

> "Religious liberty and inviolability of property," she declared, "are hereby granted to all subjects of Russia, and certainly to the Jews also; for the humanitarian principles of her Majesty do not permit the exclusion of the Jews alone from the favors shown to all, so long as they, like faithful subjects, continue to employ themselves as hitherto in commerce and handicrafts, each according to his vocation."

In 1786 a ruling was issued by the Russian Senate allowing landlords to lease businesses and inns to Jews, and permitting the election of Jews to the courts, the merchant guilds, the magistracy, and the city councils. Religious matters were placed under the jurisdiction of the rabbis and the kahals,[72] and Jews were granted protection for the exercise of their religion.

As business improved, partially as a result of this ruling, White-Russian Jews started to emigrate from White Russia to Moscow, where greater commercial opportunities existed. This aroused opposition of the Muscovite merchants who applied to the military commander of Moscow for the exclusion of the Jews, because, as they claimed, the Jews were competing unfairly. As a result, Jewish merchants were permitted to transact business but were not permitted to register in the Moscow merchant guild. Although she was liberal in her personal views, Catherine the Great was careful not to antagonize the Greek-Orthodox clergy.

In 1795, just prior to the death of Catherine the Great, Russia annexed most of the parts of Poland that had large Jewish populations.

Although Catherine the Great disliked her son Paul intensely and on several occasions had attempted to change the law of succession to his disadvantage, Paul ascended the Russian throne following his mother's death in 1796.

The reign of Paul I, who was murdered in 1801, was one of the most chaotic periods in Russian history, but it was a good period for the Jews. Paul's attitude toward the Jews was one of tolerance and kindly regard. He opposed attempts to expel the Jews from the cities and he decreed that no obstacles be placed in their way while in the pursuit of their trades or handicrafts. Perhaps his most important decision concerning the Jews was his response to the question involving the attitude of the government toward the Jewish schism that had resulted from the formation of the sect of Hasidim.

The dispute between the liberal Hasidim and the traditional rabbinic Jews had become violent. The two parties began to make false accusations against each other to the government. When his opponents accused him of attempting to injure the government, the representative of the Hasidim, Zalman Borukhovich, was arrested and taken to St. Pe-

---

72 Sometimes spelled *Qahal*, this was the name of the autonomous governments
    of Jewish communities in Eastern Europe.

tersburg. He succeeded, however, in convincing the authorities of his in-nocence. At the same time he also managed to place the Hasidim in a favorable light. He was released, and orders were issued to the rabbinic Jewish community directing that Hasidism be tolerated and that its ad-herents be left unmolested.

Paul was eventually succeeded by his son, Alexander I, who served as Emperor of Russia from 1801 to 1825. He was also King of Poland, and Grand Duke of Finland and Lithuania.

Alexander's reign was a mostly favorable one for the Jews. In 1804 he enacted laws designed to encourage the spread of modern education among the Jewish masses, and to hasten their Russification. Despite the hostility of some rabbinic Jews, the integration and political emancipa-tion of the Jews in Russia had begun with the enactment of this law.

Nicholas I succeeded to the throne in 1825, and ushered in a period of outstanding achievement in Russian literature. During his reign Nikolai Gogol, Mikhail Lermontov, Alexander Pushkin, and others wrote their finest works, and Fyodor Dostoevsky, Leo Tolstoy, Ivan Turgenev and Jewish authors Mendele Moykher Sforim, and Osip Rabbinowitz began their careers.

Jewish Society in the Eighteenth Century

By the middle of the eighteenth century the majority of European Jews had started on their way toward economic and political emancipa-tion. All of the countries in which there was a substantial Jewish popula-tion had lifted, to varying degrees, the restrictions on Jewish commerce, religious observance, education, and travel. Only those restrictions that had been, and continued to be imposed by the rabbis remained inviolate.

For the unaffiliated Jews who had been living outside of the rab-binic strictures, the new European social and educational opportunities opened a new world of communication that was based on merit rather than social station. The Academies and Learned Societies, the Republic of Letters, the Coffee Houses and Cafes, the Debating Societies, and es-pecially the Salons smoothed the way for them to enter even the highest intellectual and economic societies.

At the same time that the Jews were struggling for economic and intellectual achievement, they were also aspiring for social acceptance. Middle and upper class Jews were participating in increasing numbers in every social venue that was open to them, especially the ones that encouraged anonymity, like the contests that were sponsored by the Academies and Learned Societies. And as their numbers and acceptance grew, Jews even became the driving force in some of these institutions.

Jewish authors, composers, and performers were beginning to make an impact in the cultural world and Jewish philosophers were challenging the intellectual world. Jewish scientists[73] and mathematicians were changing the general perception of the physical world. But within the traditional nuclear rabbinic communities Talmudic study continued to be the center of their universe and contact with the outside world was discouraged.

And then, with explosive force, radical thinkers within the Jewish community began making seismic changes to Jewish religious philosophy and observance. The rabbis and their supporters fought these changes with all the weapons in their arsenal, but in the end, Hasidism, Mussar, Haskalah and their variants reshaped Judaism and the role of the rabbis.

For possibly the first time since the beginning of the rabbinic period after the destruction of the Second Temple, *popular and attractive* new forms of Judaism began to appear.

Hasidism[74]

Surprisingly, Hasidism, which is now identified with the most religious segment of the Jewish religious spectrum, was, at the time of its introduction, considered the greatest threat to the continuity of Judaism since, perhaps, the advent of Christianity. In fact, it was considered such a threat that its founder, the Ba'al Shem Tov, was excommunicated by the leader of rabbinic Judaism, the chief rabbi of Vilna.

Hasidism was based on the belief that the feeling, sentiment, and emotion of Judaism are more important than religious dogma and ritual;

---

73 For example, the Jews Adolph von Baeyer won the Nobel Prize in Chemistry in 1905, Albert Michelson won the Nobel Prize in Physics in 1907, and Paul Ehrlich won the Nobel in Medicine in 1908.

74 The word "Hasidism" means piety and thus a Hasid is a pious person.

and that it is possible to be a religious Jew without performing all the ritual or even praying. The early Hasidim believed that one's inner motives rather than one's outer religious behavior are the most important factor. Rabbinic Judaism, they claimed, had become a system of dry academic Biblical and Talmudic study filled with religious formalism. This formalism, they said, rewarded the scholars but failed to satisfy those, both learned and unlearned, who sought comfort and consolation in religion.

Hasidism welcomed the joy of spirituality by presenting a simple, more stimulating and comforting faith. In contrast to the rabbinic teachings, Hasidism did not offer dogmatic or ritual reform, but rather a deeper psychological one. It created a new type of religious mysticism that placed emotion above reason, and religious exaltation above knowledge.

Leanings toward mysticism had become common among the Jewish peasants in the scattered villages of the Ukraine[75] where they were far removed from Poland's intellectual centers. Their pervading poverty, ignorance, and superstition created a fertile field for the growth of mystical movements like Hasidism. But among the established rabbinic clergy in the cities and in urban Poland the rise of Hasidism generated new fears of apostasy. A historic struggle for supremacy was about to begin between traditional rabbinic Judaism and the new mystical spirituality offered by the HaIn many ways, because Hasidism opened the religious door to uneducated Jews, it was the most momentous spiritual revolution to affect the religious and social life of eastern European Jews since the start of the Diaspora.

Israel ben Eliezer who was known as the Ba'al Shem-Tov[76] (often abbreviated by the acronym Besht) was the founder of Hasidism. He was born in Podolia, a predominantly Ukrainian community with a large Jewish minority located in a densely populated agricultural region of Ukraine. Abba Eban, in his history, My *People, The Story of the Jews*, writes:

> In his youth he [the Ba'al Shem-Tov] is reputed to have been attracted less to Talmudic study than to the world of nature, the field and forests of his native province. Withdrawing into a life of contemplation the Besht spent several years preparing for a career as a "maker of miracles." Self

---

75 The provinces of Volhynia, Podolia, and Galicia were typical.
76 Ba'al Shem Tov literally means "bearer of a good name" and was the title used by herbalists and healers.

styled miracle workers abounded at this time in Eastern Europe. But none of them matched this young man in the intense magnetism of his personality or in the fervor of his religious faith. Long periods of mystical introspection, punctuated by visions of unearthly perfection led the Besht to abandon the vocation of faith healer and to go forth to preach the message imparted to him by the heavenly forces. His word spread like wildfire through Poland. People came in the thousands to hear him speak, to savor his words, to receive his blessing, and to join him in frenzied prayer. Here was a man who inspired them with new hope and optimism. The Besht was not a philosopher: he left behind him no theological system. Rather, he affirmed the oldest of religious truths, and in so doing struck the deepest chords of faith in the hearts of his listeners.

The Ba'al Shem Tov felt that the essence of Judaism was not in ritual and law. Though he recognized the validity of ritual, he proclaimed that the performing of ritual alone did not constitute faith. To him, the most important aspect of religion was maintaining a living relationship with God. He agreed that the most efficient means of spiritual union with God was prayer, but he felt that for the true Hasid, this meant prayer whenever one desired to pray, prayer with whatsoever words, or melodies, came to one at the moment of prayer. It was not necessary, indeed it was possibly injurious he declared, to pray at certain fixed times of the day. Prayer, the Ba'al Shem Tov proclaimed, was a matter of the heart, not of the clock; a matter, not of obligation, but of inward joy.

During his early years, the Ba'al Shem Tov was an herbalist and spent much time in the nearby forest in meditation and solitude. Around 1736, he revealed himself as a spiritual healer and a leader and in 1740, he moved closer to Lithuania. There, with a pipe in hand, he told seemingly secular tales with deep religious meanings. His talks focused far more on an individual's personal relationship with God than on the intricacies and obligations of Jewish law. As his fame spread disciples started coming to him from the surrounding countries.

The Besht was the idol of the common people. Characterized by an extraordinary sincerity and simplicity, he knew how to gain an insight into the spiritual needs of the masses. He taught them that a plain man filled with a sincere belief in God, and whose prayers come from the heart, is more acceptable to God than the rabbi versed in the Law who has spent his life absorbed in the study of the Talmud. This democratization of Judaism attracted not only the common people, but also many of the more successful unaffiliated Jews who had been excluded from the rabbinic community because of the paucity of their Talmudic and biblical learning. Even some scholars whom the rabbinical scholasticism and asceticism had failed to satisfy were drawn to Hasidism.

The rapid spread of Hasidism greatly troubled the rabbis who immediately recognized it as a dangerous enemy. The doctrine of the Besht, claiming that faith rather than religious knowledge was the true route to understanding God, was in direct opposition to the principal dogma of rabbinism, which measured man's religious value by the extent of his Talmudic learning. The ritual formalism of rabbinic Judaism, the rabbis realized, could not compete with the joy and informal spirituality of Hasidism. They saw in Hasidism a threatening competitor; one in which a charismatic lay leader could become popular and gain acolytes and a following very quickly.

A bitter struggle soon arose between the traditional rabbinic communities led by Elijah ben Solomon, the brilliant and highly respected Vilna Gaon[77] and the Hasidim. In 1772, when the first circles of Hasidim appeared in Lithuania, the Vilna Gaon, who saw himself as the guardian of learned and ritualistic Judaism, took action. As the head of the rabbinic "kahal" (council) of Vilna, he had the local leaders of Hasidism arrested and he excommunicated its adherents. Circulars were sent from Vilna to the rabbis of other communities calling upon them to make war upon the "godless sect". They resolved, at the council of rabbis held in the village of Zelva, Grodno, in 1781, to "uproot" the destructive teachings of the Besht. Their circulars ordered the faithful to expel the Hasidim from every Jewish community, to regard them as members of another faith, to hold no intercourse with them, not to intermarry with them, and not even to bury their dead[78].

But the popular strength of Hasidism was too great for the traditional rabbis and they had to reduce and eventually discontinue their opposition. In the nineteenth century the great force of Hasidism introduced a new level of religious enthusiasm into the stagnant rabbinical Judaism. It also opened the door for Jews who did not have liturgical skills

---

77 Gaon is an honorary title given to the greatest scholar of his time.

78 Non Jews may not be buried in a Jewish cemetery so this implied that the Hasidim were not Jewish.

to achieve the highest levels of communication with God. Reluctantly at first, but with increasing effect, the Rabbinic Orthodox community absorbed many of the teachings of the Ba'al Shem Tov. They eventually adapted or even co-opted many of its most basic tenets so that by the early twentieth century the Hasidism of the Besht had ceased to exist, and the word Hasidism became synonymous with Rabbinic Orthodoxy.

The Mussar Movement

The Mussar movement was a Jewish ethical movement that developed in 19th century Eastern Europe. The Hebrew word mussar means ethics and was used by the Mussar movement to refer to its efforts to encourage ethical and spiritual development both within and without the Jewish community.

The founding of the Mussar movement is attributed to Rabbi Yisrael Lipkin who was also called Rabbi Salanter[79] (1810–1883). Although he was reputed to be one of the most brilliant scholars of his time, Salanter rebelled against the rabbinic community's exaltation of Talmudic study. Salanter felt that this emphasis on Talmudic study neglected the social and emotional aspects of Judaism. Like the Hasidim, he spoke about the inadequacies of the dry intellectual exercise afforded by Talmudic studies and in 1842 he established a school in Vilna where he emphasized moral teachings based on the ethics taught in traditional Jewish rabbinic works.

Rabbi Salanter held that Jewish ethics mandated that moral behavior could supersede the laws of the Torah and that the Torah *must* be put aside in order to save lives. He set an example during the cholera epidemic of 1848 when he instructed his disciples to work on Shabbat (the Jewish Sabbath) to continue doing whatever palliative work was necessary. Despite the rabbinic prohibition against doing work on Shabbat, Salanter made certain that all the work that his Jewish disciples had been doing during the week would continue to be done by *them* rather than by non-Jewish substitutes as had been the rabbinic custom[80]. Dur-

---

79   The title *Salanter* was added to his name since most of his schooling took place in Salant (now the Lithuanian town of Salantai).

80   Rabbinic Judaism encourages the hiring of a "Shabbos Goy" (Sabbath non-Jew) prior to the Sabbath to perform the tasks that are prohibited for Jews

ing Yom Kippur (the Day of Atonement) of that year, Rabbi Salanter ordered that Jews must not abide by the traditional fast, but instead must eat in order to maintain their strength to avoid illness from the epidemic.

In 1880 Rabbi Salanter wrote about the conscious and subconscious processes and the role they play in the psychological, emotional and moral functioning of man. His writings on subconscious mind appeared well before the concept was popularized by Sigmund Freud. These concepts, which he referred to as the "outer" and "inner" processes are a fundamental element of many of Rabbi Salanter's letters, essays and teachings. He wrote that it is critical for a person to recognize what his subconscious motivations are and to work on understanding them. In this way, Rabbi Salanter replaced the mystical influence of God which had been preached for centuries by the rabbis, with rational behavior control. He urged his followers to engage in meditation in addition to, and sometimes instead of prayer, and he taught that the time for a person to work on controlling improper subconscious impulses was during times of emotional quiet, when a person is more in control of his thoughts and feelings. Rabbi Salanter stressed that when a person is experiencing an acute emotional response to an event, he is not necessarily in control of his thoughts and faculties and will not have access to the calming perspectives necessary to allow his rational mind to intercede. He wrote that,

> The busy man does evil wherever he turns. His business doing badly, his mind and strength become confounded and subject to the fetters of care and confusion. Therefore appoint a time on the Holy Sabbath to gather together at a fixed hour... the notables of the city, whom many will follow, for the study of morals. Speak quietly and deliberately without joking or irony, estimate the good traits of man and his faults, how he should be castigated to turn away from the latter and strengthen the former. Do not decide matters at a single glance, divide the good work among you — not taking up much time, not putting on too heavy a burden. Little by little, much will be gathered... In the quiet of reflection, in reasonable deliberation, each will strengthen his fellow and cure the foolishness of his heart and eliminate his lazy habits.

In many ways, the Mussar movement as described by Rabbi Salanter is similar to today's Buddhism which has been attractive to an increasingly large number of unaffiliated Jews. The Mussar movement was a

---

on the Sabbath.

timely reaction to the social changes that were occurring among Jews in the eighteenth and nineteenth century. With its focus on Jewish morality rather than religion, its declaration that inner peace could be achieved through introspection, and its emphasis on lay support rather than religious or rabbinic intercession, the Mussar movement provided a new avenue for the reconnection of formerly unaffiliated Jews. In addition, as many of the traditional religious institutions were becoming less relevant to the lives of modern nineteenth century Jews, and observance of traditional rabbinic Jewish law and custom was on the decline, the Mussar movement became an increasingly attractive alternative.

Once again, opposition to the Mussar Movement developed in large segments of the rabbinic community. The practice of meditation and the study of ethical works rather than religious observance threatened to split the community like the Hasidic movement had a century before. Many rabbis opposed Rabbi Salanter's new educational system with its emphasis on morality and inner peace. Others charged that deviations from traditional methods were heretic and would lead to assimilation.

But the commanding influence of Rabbi Salanter's personality overcame all opposition; and the Mussar movement gradually developed without producing the harmful results which had been predicted by its opponents. By the end of the 19th century most opposition to Mussar had withered away, and, like Hasidism a century earlier, many of its philosophic attitudes were accepted by much of rabbinic Jewry.

Haskalah

Maskilim, the adherents of the Haskalah movement, also known as the Jewish Enlightenment, encouraged both affiliated and unaffiliated Jews to end their religious isolation and to acquire the knowledge, customs, culture and aspirations of the nations among whom they lived. It was marked by an increase in the study of biblical Hebrew as well as both modern and traditional Hebrew literature. In this way, the Haskalah encouraged the substitution of the study of modern Jewish subjects for the study of the Talmud.

The father of the Haskalah, the German Jewish philosopher Moses Mendelssohn created a German language translation of the Torah. This translation simultaneously enabled the rabbinic Jews to learn the German language and the unaffiliated Jews to study the Bible without the intercession of the rabbis.

Fluency in the German language was necessary to secure entrance into commercial circles and Mendelssohn's translation of the Torah enabled Yiddish speaking Jews to develop a working knowledge of German. By translating the Torah, which for many centuries had served as a school-book in the early stages of a rabbinical education, Mendelssohn enabled ambitious young rabbinic Jews to enter the world of secular knowledge.

Mendelssohn's translation made study of the Torah, which had previously been restricted to Hebrew reading scholars, accessible to the unaffiliated Jews. In a further effort to make the study of the Torah accessible to non Hebrew readers, Mendelssohn supervised the writing of a German language commentary on the Torah which incorporated many of the existing rabbinic commentaries. He achieved extraordinary success by creating an educational tool that would facilitate learning wherever Jews lived rather than physically linking them to the rabbis. These books counteracted the elite and exclusionary rabbinical method of exegesis and became the primer of the Haskalah.

As long as rabbinic Jews lived in segregated communities and had limited contact with their Gentile neighbors, the rabbi remained the most influential, and often also the wealthiest, member of the Jewish community. In addition to his religious responsibilities, the rabbi was also the civil judge and often wielded other important administrative powers. For an ambitious young Jewish boy and his parents in a rabbinic community, becoming a rabbi was the highest aim, and excelling at the study of the Talmud was the means of achieving that coveted position. Nearly from birth, these young men focused on that goal and avoided the distractions of the surrounding communities. But the German language skills that these bright young Jewish men were able to achieve through the program introduced by Mendelssohn made it possible for them to seek new opportunities outside the community.

Once these young Jews became fluent in the German language they were able to move outside the segregated communities and into the rapidly growing nineteenth century cultural and economic scene. And once they moved outside the community and applied their learning skills they achieved great success in the rapidly changing secular world.

The Haskalah movement spread rapidly in Germany. It was sponsored by wealthy Jews, and Mendelssohn was its leading advocate. In Germany, the academies and salons provided literate Jews with the next step of integration and they soon attained social and intellectual prominence. In Poland and Bohemia, Jews who had been at the cradle of the Haskalah in Germany returned to their native countries to spread its tenets among their coreligionists. The "battle between light and darkness," as the Maskilim fondly described their movement, was soon raging in Bohemia and Galicia, and spreading into Russia. In Prague, as in other Austrian provinces where the German influence was strong, the Haskalah took almost the same course as in Germany. The Maskilim in the various communities were encouraged and supported by wealthy men who were outside the authority of the rabbis. These powerful advocates promoted the growth of the Haskalah and assisted in the production and dissemination of its literature.

In Russia especially, there were a number of men of wealth and position who were eager to spread the Berlin Haskalah to their respective localities. The first secular Jewish school in Russia was opened in Uman in the Ukraine, in 1822. It was conducted "after the system of Mendelssohn," and was followed in other cities, where "merchants from Brody and teachers from Tarnopol" had planted the seed of Galician Haskalah. Similar schools were established in Odessa and Kishinef, and later in Riga (1839) and Vilna (1841).

Although its intention had been to facilitate the integration of Jews into the wider society, the Haskalah also resulted in the creation of a secular Jewish culture, with an emphasis on Jewish history and Jewish identity, rather than religion. Eventually, this new secular culture led to the struggle for Jewish emancipation, involvement in new Jewish political movements, and later, the development of a Jewish Nationalism. Thus it may be said that "The emancipation of the Jews brought forth two opposed movements: the cultural assimilation, begun by Moses Mendelssohn, and Zionism, founded by Theodor Herzl in 1896."

THE NEW JUDAISM OF THE NINETEENTH CENTURY

Until the early 1800s there was only one kind of Judaism. We have been calling this Judaism *rabbinic* Judaism, but since it was the only game in town it was simply called Judaism. There were high standards required by the communities that made up rabbinic Judaism. In order for a man[81] to belong, it was necessary for him accept the superior status of scholars and the inferior status of laborers and merchants. Success in these communities was based on two disparate values: Either a man possessed a burning ambition and drive to achieve the highest level of Talmudic knowledge, or he was willing to accept total subjugation to the rabbi and the needs of the community[82]. Either way, he had to be willing to suppress his personal secular ambition in favor of religious acceptance. Members of the rabbinic communities lived under the watchful eye of the rabbi and measured their achievements by his approval which was usually based on the standards of Halacha. Jews had only two choices — there were no shades of grey — either join the rabbinic community and accept the dominance of the rabbi, or leave. Most chose to leave.

But in the early 1800s Jewish religious alternatives started to appear. These alternatives enabled uneducated Jews to affiliate with a synagogue, take courses on Jewish subjects, join Jewish social institutions, and challenge rabbinic authority without fear of being ostracized. These Jews did not have to be Talmudic scholars; they did not have to be knowledgeable about the bible or Jewish customs; they did not have to know how to read Hebrew[83], and they did not have to live within the confines of the rabbinic community. All they had to do was to be Jewish and to want to associate with other Jews.

---

81 There were no opportunities for women to excel outside of the shadow of their husbands.

82 The story Bontche Schweig by I. L. Peretz, is typical: Having died after a wretched and barren life on earth, Bontche Schweig goes to heaven for his reward. Since life has taught him to expect nothing, he expects nothing in heaven. Even when the angels turn out to honor him, he remains mute and bewildered. When he is offered anything he wants as a reward for his gentle, uncomplaining humility, he can ask only that every day he be given a hot roll with fresh butter; and even the angels are ashamed that his greatest wish is so pitiful.

83 In 1857, the year's best selling Hebrew novel sold 1200 copies; the same year a minor Yiddish novel by Isc Meir Dik sold 120,000.

And so Jews, many thousands of them, were drawn to these more modern alternative forms of Judaism. And the more that joined, the more attractive it became for the remaining unaffiliated Jews to join. Huge congregations emerged with spectacular prestigious "Temples" that were led by charismatic rabbis and offered intellectually and emotionally inspiring services. These new congregations outshone and instantly dwarfed the rabbinic communities[84]. In an effort to keep up with this new fashionable and accessible Judaism, the rabbinic communities began to modernize as well, and split into competing sects that varied in the degree of their devotion to Halacha. Even the most traditional of the rabbinic communities modernized to some extent, and imitated elements of the new temple ritual such as sermons and choirs, and the development of prayer books that were more accessible to lay people[85].

In chronological order the major new Jewish movements were the Reform Movement (1817), the Orthodox Movement (1841) and the Conservative Movement (1847).

Reform Judaism

In keeping with the philosophy of the Haskalah, some German Jewish religious leaders sought to *re-form* Jewish ritual. The leaders of this "Reform" movement organized a synagogue which incorporated music and conducted the service in German rather than Hebrew and Aramaic in order to make the service more interesting and attractive. The traditional rabbis opposed this change and they persuaded the German government to close the synagogue.

Like the Haskalah, the first reformers considered themselves an alternative within the rabbinic Jewish community that would broaden the appeal of Judaism. They did not consider themselves a separate religious group. However, as a result of the strong opposition of the rabbinic community they obtained permission from the German state to establish a separate organizational structure within the Jewish community, including unique congregations. After the establishment in 1817 of the first Re-

---

84   Even today, 80% of affiliated Jews are members of "Liberal" synagogues.
85   Prayer book changes included the insertion of instructions and the use of more interesting and varied type styles. Some even included translations into German.

form Synagogue, the "New Temple Association" of Hamburg, and the publication of its own liturgy in 1819, the movement spread very rapidly across central Europe and was the dominant Jewish denomination in Prussia, Austria-Hungary, and France by the middle of the 19th century.

During the 1840s and 1850s, reform congregations were established in two major German-Jewish centers: Frankfurt and Berlin. In 1870, with demand for Reform rabbis growing, the movement opened a rabbinical seminary and research center known as the Hochschule für die Wissenschaft des Judentums (College of Jewish Studies).

Some of the changes that the Reform congregations instituted were prayer in the local language, the acceptance of mixed seating, the change from two day holidays to single day observance, a rabbinic sermon, and the use of a professional cantor[86], choir and organ.

While it never actively proselytized gentiles, the Reform Movement's ready embrace of converts, acceptance of mixed marriages, and recognition of children of patrilineal Jewish descent increased its attractiveness to unaffiliated Jews.

The Orthodox Movement

Orthodox Judaism was developed by a group of traditionalist German Jews who supported some of the values of the Haskalah and Musar movements but who wanted to retain a traditional interpretation of Jewish law and tradition. This group was led by Rabbi Samson Raphael Hirsch who, in 1841 founded a secondary school with a curriculum featuring both Jewish and secular studies which followed his dictum, *Torah im Derech Eretz* ("The Torah is maximalised in partnership with worldly involvement"). In 1851 Hirsch became rabbi of an Orthodox separatist group in Frankfurt am Main. This group, known as the "Israelite Religious Society", had, to a great extent, accepted many philosophical aspects of classical Reform Judaism and had adopted some ritual like the shabbat morning sermon. Under Hirsch's leadership they held that Torah thought should be applied to the entire realm of human experi-

---

86 The role of the hazzan/cantor as full-time professional was originated by the Reform movement. In some German communities professionally trained hazzanim were accepted by the secular governments as clergy in the same way that rabbis were accepted as clergy.

ence—including the secular disciplines. This approach was called "neo-Orthodoxy," which subsequently became known simply as Orthodoxy. Although he insisted on strict adherence to Jewish beliefs and practices, he held that Jews should attempt to engage and influence the modern world. Unlike the rabbinic Jews, the Orthodox Jews encouraged those secular studies that were compatible with Torah thought.

In 1876 in reaction to the rapid growth of the Reform movement and the liberalization of traditional Judaism, a separate Orthodox community, officially recognized by the German government, was established. A similar organization, the Shomrei ha-Dass (Keepers of the Faith) association, was created in Hungary to combat the rapid spread of Reform Judaism in Europe. The traditionalist (rabbinic) rabbis in Germany and Hungary refused to be associated with the liberal changes to traditional ritual that were being made by the Orthodox movement and formally established what was known as Austritt, or separatist, Judaism[87].

Conservative Judaism

Rapidly following on the heels of the formation of Orthodox Judaism, Conservative Judaism took a position between the traditionalist Orthodox and the progressive Reform movements. Initially founded in Germany in the 1850s, under the title of "Historical Judaism," Conservative Judaism emerged as a moderately traditionalist response to what its founders viewed as the excessive rejection of Jewish law and rituals made by Reform Judaism. Unlike the Reform movement which based its reforms on adaptation to German social norms, the changes initiated by the Conservative movement were based on traditional Halacha. They conceived of Judaism as a historically developing religion that promoted the *conservation* of Jewish law within the context of contemporary realities. Conservative Jews claimed that it is possible to maintain (conserve) traditional Jewish elements while continuing in moderated modernization. They sought to live simultaneously in both worlds and they claimed that both the Orthodox and Reform movements were too extreme.

Like the Orthodox Jews, and in opposition to the Reform Jews, the Conservatives maintained many traditional Jewish religious observances

---

87 This schism in the Orthodox community can still be seen in the separation and competition between today's "Modern Orthodox" and "Haredi" Jews.

such as the dietary laws and the adherence to the Sabbath. Early Conservative Judaism was mainly influenced by the theology of a group of modernizing, but ritually traditionalist rabbis and Jewish historians in Germany, who founded the Judisch-Theologisches Seminar (Jewish Theological Seminary) in Breslau in 1847 in reaction to the radicalism of the early Reform movement.

While accepting the findings of modern, critical biblical scholarship, Conservative Judaism still considered the Torah to be divinely inspired, if not textually immaculate. Conservative Judaism also encouraged study of the Talmud and rabbinic sources, but treated their legal rulings more loosely than Orthodox Judaism.

Jewish Emancipation

European governments began granting the Jewish people rights as equal citizens between the late 18th century and the early 20th century through the gradual abolition of the discriminatory laws that had been applied since the middle ages specifically against Jews.

Jewish involvement in gentile society which had begun during the Age of Enlightenment accelerated in 1791 when France became the first country in Europe to emancipate its Jewish population. Holland followed in 1796, granting its Jews equal rights with gentiles. And, starting in 1799 Napoleon freed the Jews in areas he conquered in Europe (1797 — Italy; 1799 — Egypt; 1808 — Spain; 1809 — Switzerland & Austria). Napoleon emancipated the Jews from laws which restricted them to ghettos, and he expanded their rights to property, worship, and careers. Despite the anti-semitic reaction to Napoleon's policies from foreign governments and within France, he believed emancipation would benefit France by attracting Jews to the country given the restrictions they faced elsewhere. He stated "I will never accept any proposals that will obligate the Jewish people to leave France, because to me the Jews are the same as any other citizen in our country. It takes weakness to chase them out of the country, but it takes strength to assimilate them." He was seen as so favorable to the Jews that the Russian Orthodox Church formally condemned him as an "Antichrist and the Enemy of God". In 1848, the Frankfurt Parliament granted German Jews the Basic Rights of citizenship.

Although official population figures in the mid seventeen hundreds placed the world Jewish population at about one million, there had to have been many more[88]. In 1938, before the Holocaust there were sixteen million Jews in the world. This number is as accurate as possible, although, given subsequent statistics, it seems somewhat conservative[89]. It is not possible that the Jewish population could have gone from 1 million in 1750 to sixteen million less than two hundred years later.

Since we know that the 1938 figure is accurate, the 1750 population count must be incorrect. Although I have found no sources that substantially contradict this 1750 population estimate of one million, I believe that it is greatly understated. According to my calculations[90] there actually were about seven million Jews in the world in 1750, but only one million of them were the *rabbinic* Jews who were counted by the rabbis in the official census[91]. The other six million were *unaffiliated* Jews. There is no other possible explanation[92].

There has always been a large majority of Jews who were, to varying degrees, passively affiliated, unaffiliated or assimilated. Many of the Jews that we have been talking about — the Jews who were disenfranchised or disenchanted in the first few hundred years of the Common Era — remained, to varying degrees, Jews in spirit but not in practice[93]. Maybe they only attended services when it was convenient, or maybe they only attended Yom Kippur services; maybe they didn't keep kosher or maybe they did whenever they could; or maybe they refused to eat pork or shellfish; maybe they lit candles on Friday night, or maybe they used a white tablecloth Friday night; maybe they insisted that their children marry someone Jewish even though they hadn't married a Jew themselves, or maybe they just liked the collegiality of being Jewish, or secretly believed

---

88   There is a persistent superstition about counting Jews and tempting the devil that is still quite common.

89   If we were to use the nazi criteria, there probably were many more than sixteen million Jews in the world at the time of the Holocaust.

90   See appendix.

91   The primary purpose of the census was collection of taxes so the smaller the reported population, the lower the taxes.

92   See appendix.

93   There is a current Jewish population that identifies themselves as "Spiritual but not religious."

that Jews were morally or intellectually superior. But enough of them remained Jewish to keep the religion alive.

(I strongly believe that it was these "marginal" Jews that kept Judaism alive. Since the population of the rabbinic Jews remained the same, around one million, it is obvious that the normal growth within the rabbinic community was offset by defections to the "marginal" community. Since world population was growing at about 10% per century, the rabbinic community must have lost 10% of its adherents per century.)

In the nineteenth and early twentieth century, when both the public and private doors were finally opened, *millions* of these so-called unaffiliated Jews reconnected with the Jewish community. They created and peopled the huge new branches of Judaism, they joined and built impressive new synagogues, and they created powerful international Jewish organizations like B'nai Brith and Hadassah, the Hebrew Immigrant Aid Society, and the Jewish World Service, and the various Zionist organizations, and ORT[94], and the American Jewish Committee, and the Federation of Jewish Philanthropies, and the UJA and the Knights of Pythias and hundreds of other Jewish fraternal, educational, philanthropic and religious institutions. They introduced and championed new forms of Jewish religious observance that were far removed from historic rabbinic Judaism. And the force of their expansion and their commitment to fellow Jews and to humanity caused even rabbinic Judaism to bend.

The Reform, Orthodox, Conservative, Reconstructionist, Humanist, and Ethical Culture movements among many others threw their doors open wide to Jews of every religious and non-religious inclination. Jews no longer had to *qualify* in order to be accepted into Jewish institutions, all they had to do was declare their heritage. The Jews who joined these new movements were not Jews who broke away from rabbinic Judaism, in fact, the rabbinic Jewish population actually increased slightly during the nineteenth century. They were, rather, Jews who had previously been unaffiliated; there is no other way to account for the rapid growth in the populations of these new institutions.

They had been culled, honed and toughened by the trials and vicissitudes of independence, and they represented the intellectual and entre-

---

94 Organization for Rehabilitation and Training.

preneurial Jewish elite. Herbert Spencer was right when he coined the phrase "survival of the fittest"; these were, indeed, the fittest.

Starting at the end of the eighteenth century and accelerating through the nineteenth and twentieth centuries, these Jews gave the world great authors, and composers, and statesmen, and physicians, and scientists, and economists. They contributed greatly to the growth of industry and were, in many cases, the backbone of banking and finance. These unaffili-ated Jews who had lived by their wits alone for so many centuries valued their Judaism more highly than even the most committed of the rabbis, because they had to make an often highly risky social and entrepreneur-ial commitment to their religion.

THE JEWS IN THE NEW WORLD

Toward the end of the nineteenth century and during the first half of the twentieth century, the center of Judaism slowly shifted from Europe to the United States as emigration accelerated. The typical Jewish im-migrant came with one essential goal in mind: A better life.

For most, this "better life" primarily involved higher income. Fami-lies sent their best and brightest[95] to the United States with the hope that these adventurers would earn enough money to bring the rest of the family over. The new "goldene madina" (golden land) was large and the opportunities were infinite. Hard work and ambition were the key to success; and the new Jewish immigrants worked hard and long. They learned to speak English quickly; they developed self help organi-zations[96]; they organized unions[97]; they started small businesses, often starting out as peddlers; and they sought and realized opportunities wherever they occurred.

Jewish merchants fanned out across the United States and through-out the Indian territories peddling their wares and eventually establish-ing retail and distribution and manufacturing businesses throughout the

---

95   Unfortunately, in the rabbinic communities the brightest students remained and sadly became victims of the Holocaust.

96   Typical was HIAS, the Hebrew Immigrant Aid Society whose primarily function was to assist in the settlement of new Jewish immigrants.

97   The ILGWU, which pitted Jewish laborers against Jewish "bosses", was the best known.

country. Typical of this development, Isaac and Jacob Gimbel opened the first Gimbel Brothers store in Milwaukee, Wisconsin in 1887; Simon Lazarus, an ordained rabbi, opened the Lazarus Department Store in Columbus, Ohio in 1851; Aaron Meier (whose son Julius was the first Jewish governor of Oregon) and Emil Frank began Meier & Frank Department Store in Portland Oregon in 1873; Isidore and Nathan Straus bought control of Macy's and opened the Herald Square store in New York in 1902; Benjamin Altman opened B. Altman & Co. in 1865; Abraham Abraham (who also established the Brooklyn Jewish Hospital) and Joseph Wechsler started what became Abraham & Straus in 1893; Andrew Saks, a street peddler from Philadelphia, and Isador Saks opened Saks & Company in Washington, DC in 1867; Morris Rich founded M. Rich Dry Goods general store in Atlanta, GA in 1867; — Mary Ann Cohen Magnin, an accomplished seamstress and lace maker, opened a department store in San Francisco which was named for her husband Isaac Magnin in 1877; William Filene (born Wilhelm Katz) opened Filenes in Boston, MA, in 1881; A. L. Neiman and his wife Carrie Marcus Neiman founded Neiman-Marcus in Dallas, TX in 1907; and in 1923 Barney Pressman sold his wife's ring and opened Barney's, the off-price men's clothing store in New York that is now a high fashion chain.

They became the retailers of the frontier, and the financiers of the American Dream. Adolph Lewisohn, Herbert Lehman, Solomon Loeb, Jacob Schiff, and the Warburg, Straus, Goldman, Guggenheim, and Sachs families were just a few of the non-rabbinic Jews who made an impact in the nineteenth century. Perhaps, a typical story is that of Abraham Block which was recounted by David M. Markus in *The Encyclopedia of Arkansas History and Culture:* (University of Arkansas, Fayetteville, AR)

Abraham Block and his family were the first documented Jewish family to immigrate to the state of Arkansas. After a period as a successful businessman in Virginia and later in New Orleans, Block moved his family to southwest Arkansas in search of new economic opportunities. He and his sons, created a regional merchant empire with businesses in various towns in Arkansas, as well as in New Orleans, Louisiana, and at several stops along the railroad route through Texas to Houston and Dallas.

He was born on January 30, 1780, or 1781, in Schwihau, Bohemia. Around the age of twelve, Block immigrated to Richmond, Virginia, most likely in the company of an older relative or perhaps he came to live with relatives already in America. Although his early family relationships are unknown, we do know that he served in the War of 1812 in the Richmond Light Infantry Blues, earning the title of captain.

On October 2, 1811, Block married fifteen-year-old Frances "Fanny" Isaacs who was the daughter of a colonial Sephardic Jew. Although the marriage between a Sephardic Jew and an Askenazic Jew was somewhat of a mixed marriage; Block's business prospects probably contributed to the approval of the marriage by her Sephardic relatives. The couple had fourteen children, with twelve living to adulthood.

In 1823, at the age of forty-three, Block liquidated some property that had been inherited from his father-in-law and began the process of moving the family westward toward Arkansas. While Fanny was pregnant with the couple's seventh child, Block left for New Orleans to begin establishing economic ties to the area. By 1825, he had started a business in the Arkansas town of Washington, nearly five hundred miles northwest. Within a year he had summoned his family and with seven young children in tow, Fanny left for Arkansas via New Orleans in 1826. They settled into a new house in Washington, Arkansas in 1827.

Although the Blocks had strong ties to the Jewish community in New Orleans, they were unable to attract any other Jews in that community to join them in Washington. As a result, their only connections to the broader American Jewish community were periodicals and occasional business trips to New Orleans. This lack of community did not, however, diminish the Blocks' ties to Judaism. When the first congregation, Sharei Chesed, formed in New Orleans in 1827, Block joined as a founding member.

By the second generation these non-rabbinic Jews had made an impact on every aspect of American life, from commerce to the arts to the sciences. J. Robert Oppenheimer, for example, the father of the Atom Bomb, was the son of unaffiliated immigrant Jewish parents, and Leonard Bernstein, the quintessential Jewish composer and conductor who was not a practicing Jew wrote many Jewish themed compositions.

Many fled to the United States to escape Nazi persecution. Typical was Victor Gruen who was born Victor Grunbaum in a middle-class Jewish family in Vienna. He trained as an architect but was also a committed socialist. Following the German Anschluss of Austria in 1938 he was briefly arrested by the Nazi authorities and released only after friends paid a bribe. He fled the country with his wife, eventually arriving in New York City. There he worked as an architect, initially on high-class Fifth Avenue shops. During the war (he tried to enlist but was rejected by the US Army), he became a naturalized American citizen and changed his surname to Gruen.

After the war, he designed the first suburban open-air shopping facility called Northland Mall near Detroit which opened in 1954. After the success of the first project, he designed the first enclosed shopping mall in the country in Edina, Minnesota. Because he invented the modern mall, Malcolm Gladwell, writing in The New Yorker, suggested that "Victor Gruen may well have been the most influential architect of the twentieth century."

In later life Gruen turned to environmental issues, drawing up theories about ideal city forms which he described as the 'cellular city'. In 1968 he retired to his native Austria, where he founded an environmental research institute. He died in 1980.

The overwhelming majority of these immigrant achievers were unaffiliated and/or liberal Jews who struggled daily with their Jewish identity. The ultra orthodox Haredi Jews and the other extreme rabbinic sects who loudly proclaimed their Jewishness lagged far behind and eventually became dependant on the liberal and unaffiliated Jews for financial support. In spite of their high visibility and aggression, their secular and even scholastic achievements were minimal.

Because of the conscious commitment to Judaism that liberal and unaffiliated Jews chose to make, it was these Jews who kept and continue to keep Judaism alive. They, and not the ultra orthodox, are the backbone of the Jewish people.

(I grew up in an integrated Jewish community that was half Italian and half Jewish. We Jews always kept a low profile and were careful to be unostentatious. We were proud to be Jews but we didn't want to be "too

Jewish" — we didn't want to be stereotyped by the non-Jews. A favorite expression of my parents was, "it's a shanda for the goyim," meaning, it's an embarrassment in front of the gentiles. Even today, when I read about a criminal, my first inclination is to check if the person is Jewish.)

Today's ultra orthodox Jewish communities are, when measured by their exclusionary policies[98], the closest equivalent to the rabbinic Jewish communities of the middle ages. In fact, the men's unique clothing, especially on the Sabbath, is an effort to imitate the dress of their successful seventeenth century Jewish communities in Poland. But surprisingly, even with their explosive birth rate, and the extraordinary subsidies granted to them by the Israeli[99] government fewer than 10% of the Jewish population considers themselves "traditional" orthodox Jews compared to an estimated 15% of the Jewish population in 1750. There are only a little over one million ultra orthodox Jews in the world — about the same number as the number of rabbinic Jews throughout the history of the Diaspora. There are well over twelve million other Jews who, though they and the rest of the world consider themselves Jewish, are, to varying degrees, not considered Jewish by the Ultra Orthodox Haredi Jews.

Recent polls have indicated that there are additional, uncounted and less clearly defined Jewish populations. There are, for example, Jews who call themselves "Jewbu",[100] and there are Jews who describe themselves as "spiritual but not religious", there are atheists and agnostics who are culturally Jewish but choose not to identify themselves as Jews, and there is a passive group of Jewish by birth "none of the above". There are also those who might be called Jewish wannabees, like Arizona Congresswoman Gabrielle Giffords, or public figures like Madonna, Marilyn Monroe, Elizabeth Taylor, and Sammy Davis Jr. who consider themselves Jewish although they possess limited, and in some circles questionable, Jewish heritage. Even the messianic movements like "Jews for Jesus" number Jews among their members and have occasionally also served as conduits for the conversion of non-Jews to Judaism. Catriel Sugarman, a researcher on Jewish issues, writes in *The Jewish Voice* (February 2009),

---

98 Especially their unique clothing requirements and behavioral restrictions
99 and to some extent the US government through tax exemptions and relief payments
100 Jewish Buddhists or Buddhist Jews

Sometimes, Gentiles who are genuinely attracted to Judaism, wind up in Messianic congregations, only as way stations before continuing on to full halachic conversion. Others decide to renounce Christianity and satisfy themselves as Noahides, believers in the One Jewish G-d who, because they do not convert, are mandated to obey only seven commandments instead of 613.

A good example is Patricia Power, who serves as undergraduate academic advisor in the religious studies department at Arizona State University. Four years ago, she converted to Judaism after years of intensive self-study of Torah and Biblical Hebrew while a member of a local Messianic group. Born and raised a Catholic, she joined a Bible church after getting married until friends invited her to join their "Messianic synagogue."

"Judaism spoke to me academically, intellectually, and spiritually; this was not anticipated by the Evangelical movement," she said.

Spiritual vs. Religious

What religion a man shall have is a historical accident,
quite as much as what language he shall speak. —George
Santayana, *Reason in Religion*

There is one final question that demands an answer: Why be Jewish? Why, after thousands of years of oppression, after suffering the greatest genocide in history, after being beaten and tortured, after being derided by both rulers and peasants, after being discriminated against in every phase of human endeavor, after suffering repeated exclusion and victimization; why after all this, would anyone want to be Jewish?

The Chuetas[101] of Majorca are probably one of the best known examples of this perseverance and dedication. When the Inquisition was established in Majorca in 1488, it granted a general amnesty to all Jews who converted to Christianity. According to the Jewish Encyclopedia, six hundred and eighty Jewish families converted and the Church agreed to receive them on payment of a considerable fine. But many of these Jews secretly retained their Jewish customs and passed them on to their children. It was not until three centuries later, in 1782, that the decree was lifted and Jews were permitted to reside in any street in the city of Palma and in any part of the island. Three years later they were declared eligible to enter the army and the navy as well as to hold public offices.

---

101 The origin of this term is obscure. Some say it refers to the Spanish word for pork; others say it is a slang for Jewish.

But to all appearances, the Chuettas had disappeared and it wasn't until late in the twentieth century that some of these families were daring enough to honestly reveal their identities. Today, some of these families are exploring opportunities to reenter the Jewish community.

Throughout the Common Era, even into the "enlightened" twenty-first century, Jews continue to be victimized, derided, and often outright hated. In many parts of the world anti-Zionism is used to camouflage latent anti-Semitism. Valerie Strauss and Emily Wax, writing in *The Washington Post*, (February 25, 2002), report that Islamic schools in Virginia have maps of the Middle East in their classrooms that are missing Israel. On one map, Israel was blackened out and replaced with "Palestine." An 11th grade textbook teaches that one sign of the Day of Judgment will be that Muslims will fight and kill Jews, who will hide behind trees that say, "Oh Muslim, Oh servant of God, here is a Jew hiding behind me. Come here and kill him."

Moslem countries openly call for the death of all Jews. As Bernard Lewis[102], writes in *The Middle East Quarterly*,

> [To] an astonishing degree, the ideas, the literature, even the crudest inventions of the Nazis and their predecessors have been internalized and Islamized. The major themes—poisoning the wells, the invented Talmud quotations, ritual murder, the hatred of mankind, the Masonic and other conspiracy theories, taking over the world—remain; but with an Islamic, even a Qur'anic twist.

> The more consistent European-type anti-Semites offer an alternative view; that America is the tool of Israel, rather than the reverse, an argument backed by a good deal of Nazi-style or original Nazi documentation. In much of the literature produced by the Islamic organizations, the enemy is no longer defined as the Israeli or the Zionist; he is simply the Jew, and his evil is innate and genetic, going back to remote antiquity. A preacher from Al-Azhar University explains in an Egyptian newspaper that he hates the Jews because they are the worst enemies of the Muslims and have no moral standards, but have chosen evil and villainy. He concludes: "I hate the Jews so as to earn a reward from God."

Even in the United States, country clubs, hotels, some industries, and even entire communities discriminate against Jews. A 2005 paper from

---

102 Bernard Lewis is Cleveland E. Dodge Professor of Near Eastern Studies Emeritus at Princeton University. He received the 1998 Ataturk International Peace Award.

the United States Commission on Civil Rights reports the following findings:

- Many college campuses throughout the United States continue to experience incidents of anti-Semitism, a serious problem warranting further attention
- When severe, persistent or pervasive, this behavior may constitute a hostile environment for students in violation of Title VI of the Civil Rights Act of 1964
- Anti-Israeli or anti-Zionist propaganda has been disseminated on many campuses that include traditional anti-Semitic elements, including age-old anti-Jewish stereotypes and defamation.
- Anti-Semitic bigotry is no less morally deplorable when camouflaged as anti-Israelism or anti-Zionism
- Substantial evidence suggests that many university departments of Middle East studies provide one-sided, highly polemical academic presentations and some may repress legitimate debate concerning Israel.
- Many college students do not know what rights and protections they have against anti- Semitic behavior.

And, as Malcolm Gladwell writes in The New Yorker, many colleges historically had quotas limiting the number of Jewish students.

> In 1905, Harvard College adopted the College Entrance Examination Board tests as the principal basis for admission, which meant that virtually any academically gifted high-school senior who could afford a private college had a straightforward shot at attending. By 1908, the freshman class was seven per cent Jewish, nine per cent Catholic, and forty-five per cent from public schools, an astonishing transformation for a school that historically had been the preserve of the New England boarding-school complex known in the admissions world as St. Grottlesex.

> As the sociologist Jerome Karabel writes in The Chosen (Houghton Mifflin, 2005), his remarkable history of the admissions process at Harvard, Yale, and Princeton, that meritocratic spirit soon led to a crisis. The enrollment of Jews began to rise dramatically. By 1922, they made up more than a fifth of Harvard's freshman class. The administration and alumni were up in arms. Jews were thought to be sickly and grasping, grade-grubbing and insular. They displaced the sons of wealthy Wasp alumni, which did not bode well for fund-raising. A. Lawrence Lowell, Harvard's president in the nineteen-twenties, stated flatly that too many Jews would destroy the school: "The summer hotel that is ruined by admitting Jews meets its fate

. . . because they drive away the Gentiles, and then after the Gentiles have left, they leave also."

Israel, the Jewish State, has been the object of governmental and academic prejudice, scorn, derision and hostility as can be seen by the recent UN efforts to delegitimize Israel.

Although Jews in Russia and in many countries of the former Soviet Union are now permitted to practice their religion, official anti-Semitism is still too common. Recently, members of the Moscow State Duma and other prominent figures expressed anti-Semitic sentiments in a January 2005 letter, urging the prosecutor general to investigate Jewish organizations and initiate proceedings to ban them, charging that a Russian translation of ancient Jewish law, the Kitzur Shulchan Arukh, incited hatred against non-Jews. According to the Anti Defamation League, in 2006 human rights organizations made numerous unsuccessful attempts to prosecute the authors of this "Letter of 500."

The few remaining Jews still living in the Arab countries live in constant fear for their lives and livelihoods. Emergency evacuations were necessary to save the lives of the Jews of North Africa. Anti Semitic graffiti is common throughout Europe. Throughout the world, synagogues and other Jewish institutions have to be protected by local police.

For some fanatically dedicated and devoted Jews, the opportunity to suffer for their religion and even die for it is considered a test from God. But for the others, the vast majority of whom live in the everyday world of latent anti-Semitism and hostility, why do they continue to be Jewish? Why don't they convert to another, more acceptable religion? Or why don't they just give up religion altogether?

And finally, why, in this twenty-first century with so many intellectual opportunities and so many less onerous alternatives, do 55% of American Jews who do not belong to a synagogue, still identify themselves as being Jewish?

Are they just caught up in the momentum or inertia of their Jewishness? Or is there something more? Something powerful and compelling that draws these people to Judaism?

Perhaps the following analysis of the psyche and lifestyle of Jewish Russian and Israeli US immigrants, which is excerpted from an article by Liel Liebovitz in *Tablet Magazine* (Dec 7, 2010), provides some clues to the motivation and rationale of modern unaffiliated Jews:

> A new influx of Jewish immigrants is reshaping American Jewish life by presenting a Jewish identity that is, for the most part, self-confident and secure. Many of these immigrants are Israeli; many more come from the former Soviet Union. For them, the familiar conundrums and existential challenges of intermarriage, dwindling synagogue attendance, and declining religious affiliation among young Jews are less important than a modern-day version of the stubborn old-school ethnic pride that the American Jewish community had largely abandoned once the gates to mainstream American institutions swung open.

> [The American Jewish Community, which was] primarily constructed around religious denominations... has little place for people who, like Israelis, have grown up divorcing Jewish identity from religious practice, or who, like Russians, have grown up in societies that forbade the study and practice of religion. For American Jews, being Jewish is a complicated undertaking woven into a long history of fear and pride and doubt and desire. For Israelis, and for Russians, it's simply something that you are, something that you do, something that requires less thought than action.

Throughout the Common Era unaffiliated Jews have continued to identify themselves as Jewish, yet they have continued to bypass the doors of institutional Judaism just as the Israeli and Russian immigrants are doing today. Some few have entered the main stream. Most have chosen to remain outside of traditional Judaism. But even though they are not part of the traditional structure, they choose to remain Jews. They could have done otherwise in the past. They certainly can do otherwise today. Do they fear the wrath of God? I doubt it. Do they fear the wrath of their parents? Not likely.

So what is the attraction?

The simple answer is that these people are Jewish because they like being Jewish. Perhaps a future study of the Jewish community should try to determine why so many unaffiliated and uncommitted Jews *choose to remain Jewish.*

I suspect that the answer will be that they see being Jewish as a special unique identity that is reserved for the "chosen" few; that it is desirable precisely because it is so visible and so often derided, and that

that derision emanates, in great measure, from people who are jealous of the unique character, perseverance, and continuity of the Jewish people. Mark Twain, who had a history of personal anti-Semitism, concluded his long and occasionally seemingly bigoted article, "Concerning the Jews" in Harpers Magazine in 1899 with the following laudatory paragraph:

> [If] the statistics are right, the Jews constitute but one per cent of the human race. It suggests a nebulous dim puff of star-dust lost in the blaze of the Milky Way. Properly the Jew ought hardly to be heard of; but he is heard of, has always been heard of. He is as prominent on the planet as any other people, and his commercial importance is extravagantly out of proportion to the smallness of his bulk. His contributions to the world's list of great names in literature, science, art, music, finance, medicine, and abstruse learning are also away out of proportion to the weakness of his numbers. He has made a marvelous fight in this world, in all the ages; and has done it with his hands tied behind him. He could be vain of himself, and be excused for it. The Egyptian, the Babylonian, and the Persian rose, filled the planet with sound and splendor, then faded to dream-stuff and passed away; the Greek and the Roman followed, and made a vast noise, and they are gone; other peoples have sprung up and held their torch high for a time, but it burned out, and they sit in twilight now, or have vanished. The Jew saw them all, beat them all, and is now what he always was, exhibiting no decadence, no infirmities of age, no weakening of his parts, no slowing of his energies, no dulling of his alert and aggressive mind. All things are mortal to the Jew; all other forces pass, but he remains. What is the secret of his immortality?

Jews are the most philanthropic: A 2003 report by Dr. Gary Tobin and colleagues at the Institute for Jewish and Community Research examined the 865 philanthropic gifts of $10 million or more made by all American donors between 1995 and 2000. Nearly twenty five percent (188 gifts totaling $5.3 billion) were made by Jews.

Jews have the highest level of intellectual achievement: One hundred and eighty-one Jews have won Nobel prizes — over twenty two percent of all the prizes awarded.

Jews are civic minded: Jews, who make up about two percent of the U.S. adult population, accounted for eight percent of the 111th Congress as a whole and twelve percent of the Senate.

Charles Murray, writing in the April 2007 issue of *Commentary Magazine*, notes that from the time of Jewish emancipation in the nineteenth century Jews [started] appearing in the first ranks of the arts and sciences. During the four decades from 1830 to 1870, when the first Jews to live under emancipation reached their forties, 16 significant Jewish figures appear. In the next four decades, from 1870 to 1910, the number jumps to 40. During the next four decades, 1910–1950, despite the contemporaneous devastation of European Jewry, the number of significant figures almost triples, to 114.

To get a sense of the density of accomplishment these numbers represent, I will focus on 1870 onward, after legal emancipation had been achieved throughout Central and Western Europe. How does the actual number of significant figures compare to what would be expected given the Jewish proportion of the European and North American population? From 1870 to 1950, Jewish representation in literature was four times the number one would expect. In music, five times. In the visual arts, five times. In biology, eight times. In chemistry, six times. In physics, nine times. In mathematics, twelve times. In philosophy, fourteen times.

Murray goes on to point out that by the measurement standard of the Nobel Prize, disproportionate Jewish accomplishment in the arts and sciences continues to this day.

In the first half of the 20th century, despite pervasive and continuing social discrimination against Jews throughout the Western world, despite the retraction of legal rights, and despite the Holocaust, Jews won 14 percent of Nobel Prizes in literature, chemistry, physics, and medicine/physiology. In the second half of the 20th century, when Nobel Prizes began to be awarded to people from all over the world, that figure rose to 29 percent. So far, in the 21st century, it has been 32 percent. Jews constitute about two-tenths of one percent of the world's population. You do the math.

Murray wonders what accounts for this remarkable record, and he concludes that although the unique character of Jewish culture might contribute, intelligence has to be at the center of the answer. Jews, Murray points out, have been found to have an unusually high mean intelligence as measured by IQ tests. The IQ mean for the American population is "normed" to be 100, with a standard deviation of 15. It is currently accepted that the Jewish mean IQ is somewhere in the range of 107 to 115, with 110 being a plausible compromise. Underlying that Jewish mean of 110 is a consistent pattern on IQ subtests: Jews are only about average on the subtests measuring visuo-spatial skills, but extremely high on subtests that measure verbal and reasoning skills.

A group's mean intelligence is important in explaining outcomes such as mean educational attainment or mean income. The key indicator for predicting exceptional accomplishment (like winning a Nobel Prize) is the incidence of exceptional intelligence. Consider an IQ score of 140 or higher, denoting the level of intelligence that can permit people to excel in fields like theoretical physics and pure mathematics. If the mean Jewish IQ is 110 and the standard deviation is 15, then the proportion of Jews with IQs of 140 or higher is somewhere around six times the proportion of everyone else.

The imbalance, as Murray points out, continues to increase for still higher IQs. In 1954, a New York psychologist used IQ test results to iden-tify all 28 children in the New York public-school system with measured IQs of 170 or higher. Of those 28, 24 were Jews. Thus, a randomly selected Jew has a higher probability of possessing that level of intelligence than a randomly selected member of any other ethnic or national group, by far.

Exceptional intelligence though, is not enough to explain the level of Jewish accomplishment. Qualities such as imagination, ambition, perseverance, and curiosity separate the merely smart from the highly productive.

Although a person must be very smart to have even a chance of achiev-ing great work, it was the unique Jewish character of toughness com-bined with ambition and intellectual curiosity that had been developed by the unaffiliated True Jews during the harsh millennia-long winter of their existence that honed their unique skills. This powerful combina-tion continues to drive today's Jews to new heights of achievement in the sciences, arts, and in every aspect of human ambition and humanitarian achievement.

IDENTIFYING THE TRUE JEW

Many rulings have been made by the ultra orthodox community re-garding the standards that they have proclaimed as necessary to identify a True Jew. They have established criteria based on matrilineal descent and they critically scrutinize every Jew's lineage to determine purity. If they discover a non Jewish matrilineal ancestor, they declare that the person is not Jewish and they require that person to undergo a conver-sion procedure overseen by an approved rabbi. But, as we have seen, modern day genetic studies clearly indicate that very few, if any, Jews have genetic purity. In fact, there is clear evidence of matrilineal *impurity*.

The question of modern day Jewish authenticity is further compli-cated by the bifurcation of lineage. Orthodox Jews determine Jewish biological identity by matrilineal analysis, while Ashkenazi Jewish social identity is designated by patrilineal naming[103]. Given the overwhelming genetic evidence, it is highly unlikely that there is such a thing as a genetically "True Jew" — a Jew who can claim genetic purity — one who can claim connection to Moses, or Mount Sinai, or the priests of the Temple, or even the authors of the Talmud.

Several recent studies[104] suggest that Jewishness has deep genetic roots. In what its authors claim is the most comprehensive study thus far, a team led by geneticist Harry Ostrer of the New York University School of Medicine concluded that three Jewish groups—Middle Eastern, Sephardic, and Ashkenazi—share genome-wide genetic markers that distinguish them from other worldwide populations.

Ostrer and his colleagues analyzed nuclear DNA from blood samples taken from a total of 237 Ashkenazi and Middle Eastern Jews in New York City, and Sephardic Jews in Seattle, Washington; Greece; Italy; and Israel. They compared these with DNA from about 2800 presumably non-Jewish individuals from around the world. The team used several analytical approaches to calculate how genetically similar the Jewish groups were to each other and to the non-Jewish groups, including a method called identity by descent (IBD), which is often used to determine how closely two individuals are related.

Individuals within each Jewish group had high levels of IBD, roughly equivalent to that of fourth or fifth cousins. *Each of the three Jewish groups also showed substantial genetic admixture (interbreeding) with nearby non-Jews.* Although Ashkenazi Jews clustered more closely with Middle Eastern and Sephardic Jews, their genetic profiles still indicate between 30% and 60% admixture with Europeans.

To repeat, this genetic analysis indicates that there has been a substantial admixture of as much as thirty to sixty percent with non Jewish Europeans. This makes it statistically unlikely that there is genetic Jewish purity within the general Jewish population including the ultra orthodox.

---

103 All Jewish children, both male and female, are given a "Hebrew" name which indicates their father — such as "Isaac, the son of Abraham." In this way, family names are continued and paternal lineage is perpetuated.

104 See Balter, Michael. "Tracing the Roots of Jewishness," *Science Now*, June 3, 2010, Sciencemag.org.

Another criterion that might be considered in determining a True Jew is seniority and historic longevity. Although this seems like a good measurement, it has never been espoused by the ultra orthodox community because the ultra orthodox community is a relative newcomer on the Jewish religious scene. Their arrival coincided with the establishment of the Pharisees as the arbiters of Judaism about two thousand years ago. But Judaism is much older than that. Some Jews, like perhaps the Jews of Persia (Iran) come closer to being historically True Jews because they have survived as a community since the destruction of the First Temple. Populations, like the Jews of southern Russia who trace their origins back to Nebuchadnezzar; or the Rabbinite and Karaite communities of the northern Black Sea coast, who trace their history back to the beginning of the Common Era; or the black and brown Jews of Algeria, Cameroon, Morocco, Syria, Tunisia, Yemen and Egypt who trace their origins to biblical times; or the Bene Israel, Cochin and Bnei Menashe communities of India; or the or the Juhurim of the eastern Caucasus, or the Kaifeng Jews of China; or the Beta Israel and Lemba of Africa, who all trace their Jewish history much further back than the ultra orthodox.

Unfortunately, the genetic study by Ostrer and his colleagues does not address the status of any of the above groups many of whose claims to Jewishness has been challenged by the haredi Jews, but additional scientific research, based on the discovery that a majority of present-day Jewish Kohanim[105] either share or are only one step removed from a pattern of markers which researchers named the Cohen Modal Haplotype (CMH), supports the claim of some of these far flung Jewish communities.

Following the discovery of the very high prevalence of 6/6 CMH matches amongst Cohens, other communities were quick to look for it and identify it as a signpost for possible Jewish ancestry. News of 6/6 matches in the Lemba of Southern Africa were seen as confirming a possible Jewish lineage; possible links were discussed between the Jews and the Kurds; and some suggested that 4/4 matches in non-Jewish Italians might be a genetic inheritance from Jewish slaves, deported by Emperor Titus in large numbers after the fall of the Temple in 70 C.E.

---

105 Priests whose ancestors were said to officiate at the Temple.

Dr. Karl Skorecki, a nephrologist and a researcher at the University of Toronto and the Rambam-Technion Medical Center in Haifa, is generally credited with the discovery of the Kohen gene[106]. The following anecdote, which was intended to show the interrelationship of Kohanim, also emphasizes the absence of a physical interrelationship among Jews in general. The italics are mine:

> Dr. Karl Skorecki was attending services one morning. The Torah was removed from the ark and a Kohen was called for the first aliya. The Kohen called up that particular morning was a visitor: a Jew of Sefardic background. His parents were from Morocco. Skorecki also has a tradition of being a Kohen, though of Ashkenazi background. His parents were born in Eastern Europe. Karl (Kalman) Skorecki looked at the Sefardi Kohen's physical features and considered his own physical features. *They were significantly different in stature, skin coloration and hair and eye color. Yet both had a tradition of being Kohanim — direct descendants of one man — Aharon HaKohen.*

> Dr. Skorecki considered, "According to tradition, this Sefardi and I have a common ancestor. Could this line have been maintained since Sinai, and throughout the long exile of the Jewish people?" As a scientist, he wondered, could such a claim be tested?

Since Jewish identity is based on matrilineal descent the question of Jewish authenticity must focus on the conversion process. This question is difficult and convoluted. As Doctor Skorecki observed, "[The Kohanim] were significantly different in stature, skin coloration, and hair and eye color." Genetic evidence clearly points to greater genetic ties among the men than among the women. Historically, Jewish men who sought to marry non-Jewish women required that they first convert to Judaism, or in some cases non-Jewish women who sought Jewish spouses voluntarily converted to Judaism. Thus, although these formerly non-Jewish converts espoused Judaism, their genetic ties were to their non-Jewish community, and their physical characteristics were those of the local community.

The process of conversion into Judaism in the twenty-first century is cumbersome and exclusionary. In the case of ultra orthodox conversions it is also very selective. It was not always this way. In the first centuries of the Common Era conversion to Judaism was encouraged and, accord-

---

106 The question of lineage of Kohanim is further complicated by the requirement that both parents of a Kohen, be Kohanim.

ing to the Jewish Encyclopedia, the primary criterion was a willingness to give up idol worship.

> The details of the act of reception seem not to have been settled definitely before the second Christian century. From the law that proselyte and native Israelite should be treated alike the inference was drawn that circumcision, and the bath of purification were [the only] prerequisites for conversion.

> Subsequently, around the third century, the concept of a bet din was added in order to avoid frivolous conversions.

> After the Hadrianic rebellion the following procedure came into use. A complete "court," or "board," of rabbinical authorities was alone made competent to sanction the reception. The candidate was first solemnly admonished to consider the worldly disadvantages and the religious burdens involved in the intended step. He, or she, was asked, "What induces thee to join us? Dost thou not know that, in these days, the Israelites are in trouble, oppressed, despised, and subjected to endless sufferings?" If he replied, "I know it, and I am unworthy to share their glorious lot," he was reminded most impressively that while a heathen he was liable to no penalties for eating fat or desecrating the Sabbath, or for similar trespasses, but as soon as he became a Jew, he must suffer excision for the former, and death by stoning for the latter. On the other hand, the rewards in store for the faithful were also explained to him. If the applicant remained firm, he was circumcised in the presence of three rabbis, and then led to be baptized; but even while in the bath he was instructed by learned teachers in the graver and the lighter obligations which he was undertaking. After this he was considered a Jew. The presence of three men was required also at the bath of women converts, though due precautions were taken not to affront their modesty. This procedure is obligatory at the present time, according to the rabbinical codes.

The Jewish Encyclopedia continues,

> In modern times [this was written around 1900] conversions to Judaism are not very numerous. Marriage is, in contravention of the rabbinical caution, in most instances the motive, and proselytes of the feminine sex predominate. In some of the new rituals formulas for the reception of proselytes are found—for instance, in Einhorn's "Olat Tamid." Instruction in the Jewish religion precedes the ceremony, which, after circumcision and baptism, consists in a public confession of faith, in the main amounting to a repudiation of certain Christian dogmas, and concluding with the reciting of the Shema'. Some agitation occurred in American Jewry over the abrogation of circumcision in the case of an adult neophyte ("milat gerim"). I. M. Wise made such a proposition before the Rabbinical Conference at Philadelphia (Nov., 1869), but his subsequent attitude on the question leaves it doubtful whether he was in earnest in making the prop-

osition. Bernard Felsenthal (Chicago, 1878) raised the question about ten years later, arguing in favor of the abrogation of the rite and quoting R. Joshua's opinion among others. The Central Conference of American Rabbis finally, at the suggestion of I. M. Wise, resolved not to insist on milat gerim, and devised regulations for the solemn reception of proselytes. I. S. Moses has proposed the establishment of congregations of semiproselytes, reviving, as it were, the institution of the ger toshab.

At the start of rabbinic Judaism changes were made to the conversion process to make it increasingly onerous, but twentieth century Orthodox rabbis have set the hurdle to conversion much higher than it ever was historically. The bible clearly deals with conversion and recommends a hospitable attitude toward the "stranger." throughout the centuries, various criteria were attached to the process of conversion, but they were usually much less stringent that today's orthodox requirements and they were not at all consistent. With the Jewish communities dispersed throughout the known world, there was neither a central authority nor a consistent set of rules regarding conversion. This means that not all Jews, even the most religious, who claim linear authenticity, are, in fact, Jewish according to today's standards as set by the ultra Orthodox. Rabbi Harold M. Schulweis puts it this way: "One of the unique aspects of Judaism is its rejection of Judaism as a biological entity, an inherited spiritual DNA, racial or ethnic. The point is that being a Jew is not a matter of genes and chromosomes. To the contrary, Judaism is the first religion to recognize the "ger," the stranger who chooses to identify himself with Judaism. Judaism is not rooted in race or clan or in a genetic matter but a religious tradition of choice."[107]

An essay in an on-line publication by Aish HaTorah, the ultra orthodox outreach group called Why *the Jews, The Racial Theory*, (international. aish.com/seminars/whythejews) writes: "Jews are not a race. *Anyone can become a Jew* — and members of every race, creed and color in the world have done so at one time or another. There is no distinguishing racial physical feature common only to Jews."

Thus, it is safe to say, that based on historic and scientific evidence there is no such thing as a full blooded, authentic, historically verifiable Jew. In addition to the main steam, there are Jews who are Unitarians,

---

107   Keruv, "Conversion and the Unchurched", Outreach Lecture I.

Secular Humanists, Ethical Culturists, Buddhists, Deists, Atheists and Agnostics. They are historically Jewish and although they are not currently being counted as Jews, they exist, and they can be just as authentically Jewish as the Haredis. All they have to do is declare their Jewishness. And if the opportunity presents itself and if the atmosphere is sufficiently hospitable they will "magically" appear as they did in the nineteenth century, and the world Jewish population will experience another unexplained growth spurt.

Chapter 3. The Bottom Line — Avoiding the Same Old Same Old

The New Judaism

There should have been a fanfare at the end of the last chapter. It should have proclaimed "Jewish world take note — and don't make the same mistakes again!"

But there was no fanfare and the Jewish world did not take note and the Jewish world is making the same mistakes again — and the world Jewish population is once again shrinking — maybe not yet in absolute numbers, but certainly in relative rate of growth.

Once again Judaism, which had flourished for two centuries, is reverting to the confining directives of the ultra orthodox Rabbis who proclaim that strict religious observance, Talmudic study, and Halachic immersion outweigh all other aspects of Judaism.

In the same way that the destruction of the Temple and the dispersion of the Jewish infrastructure in 70 CE led to the development of rabbinic Judaism, the Holocaust with its severe loss of Jewish scholars was the indirect cause of this reversion to rabbinic Judaism.

There was a horrific and disproportionate loss of Jewish scholars in the Holocaust. Some theories hold that because of the insular nature of their community and their need to live within the confines of a closed religious society, rabbinic Jews suffered the highest percentage of loss in the Holocaust. Because of their inability to quickly abandon the support system of their community, they were an easy target for the Nazis.

The surviving Jews, who had been more mobile and thus more able to escape, were determined to recover from the ravages of the Holocaust. And so, they elevated the remaining scholars and their disciples to the level of "untouchables." In Israel special status[108] was given to rabbinic schools and their students. In the US massive amounts of money flowed from the liberal Jewish community into yeshivas that were specially created to resurrect the lost rabbinic heritage. Slowly sacred books were recovered; teachers were found, and a new group of scholars was born.

In an effort to re-establish the unique character of the rabbinic communities, these scholars affected eighteenth century European clothing styles. The women covered their heads and wore distinctly identifiable clothing. Although they were, for the most part, born in the United States, they chose to speak Yiddish, the historic language of the shtetle, in their homes rather than their native English. The men grew impressive beards, some wore spats and striped suits, some wore fancy fur hats, some wore prayer shawls over their clothing, and some wore all of these and more. They prohibited the introduction of twentieth century media into their homes, and some even discouraged their children from speaking English.

The effect was to isolate themselves from the general Jewish population.

And then slowly, imperceptibly at first, and then with shocking speed and audacity they presented themselves as the *only authentic Jews*. Somehow the perceptions changed and the more secular Jews who had sustained and nourished the Jewish religion for two centuries, those same liberal Jews who had provided funds and opportunities to resurrect the downtrodden scholars, were now portrayed by those very scholars as second class non-authentic Jews.

And so, today, seventy years after the Holocaust, barely two hundred years after the historic growth and unification of the Jewish People that we talked about in the last chapters, the Jews are making the same mis-

---

108   This included a learning stipend, tax free status and waiving of the universal military duty obligation.

takes, with the same consequences. Consider this July 13, 2010 article by Janine Zacharia in the Washington Post:

> JERUSALEM — An Israeli parliamentary committee on Monday advanced a bill that could lead to lack of recognition for conversions to Judaism performed by rabbis from the Reform and Conservative movements.
>
> The bill could give the chief rabbinate, the religious authority in Israel run by ultra-Orthodox Jews, the power to decide which conversions are accepted, overturning an Israeli Supreme Court decision that ensures eligibility for Israeli citizenship for Jews converted by rabbis from all branches of Judaism.
>
> Representatives of the Reform and Conservative movements, which have been battling for years for more rights in Israel, saw the committee vote as a threat to their efforts to strengthen their legitimacy in Israel. The chief rabbinate already holds a monopoly on such rituals as marriage and divorce.
>
> "It sets us back 20 years in terms of the advances that were made," said Rabbi Steven Wernick, executive vice president of the United Synagogue of Conservative Judaism, an umbrella organization of Conservative Jewish congregations in the United States, who spoke by telephone during a visit to Jerusalem. "The practical implication of this bill is one that we are very, very concerned about and angry about."
>
> The bill "delegitimizes most of North American Jewry" and brings back the question of "who has the authority to determine someone's Jewish identity," Wernick added, noting that 85 percent of American Jewry is affiliated with non-Orthodox branches of Judaism.

The results of this reestablishment of Jewish stratification and the disenfranchisement of a large portion of the Jewish population have been sudden and severe. Disenfranchised Jews of all ages are leaving the fold in droves. The following is from the United Jewish Communities' National Jewish Population Survey:

> As previous analyses have shown and the NJPS data confirm, the intermarriage rate among American Jews climbed dramatically over the course of the second half of the twentieth century. The intermarriage rate for Jews who married before 1970 stands at 13%, rises to 28% for those whose marriages started in the 1970s, and then increases again to 38% for Jews married in the first half of the 1980s.
>
> [Among] Jews whose marriages started in 1985-90, the intermarriage rate is 43%. The intermarriage rate is also 43% for Jews whose marriages be-

gan in 1991-95. Jews who have married since 1996 have an intermarriage rate of 47%.

Although the right wing (ultra) Orthodox movement claims the mantle of authenticity, they represent only a small percentage of the smallest of the three major Jewish denominations. The 1990 National Jewish Population Survey of the Council of Jewish Federations reported that only 6.8% of Jews describe themselves as Orthodox, and only a fraction of those self-described Orthodox Jews are in the Ultra Orthodox community.[109]

In Israel, although they have high visibility and, as a result of their political clout, have a disproportionate impact on Israeli society, the Haredi (ultra orthodox) community is only 10% of the population. Due to youthful marriage and their prohibition against contraception and the consequent high birth rate, the ultra orthodox population is growing faster than both the general Jewish population and the general population. But this rapidly growing Haredi population is not economically self sustaining and cannot continue to exist without the very substantial financial support of the government and the non Orthodox community. The National Jewish Population Study of 2000-20001 notes (italics are mine):

> Jews[110] continue to display extraordinary achievement in terms of educational attainment, occupational prestige and household income. These achievements underlie and promote cultural sophistication, communal involvement, and influence in the public square. *They infuse Jewish communal institutions with significant resources — intellectual talent, financial assets and civic influence — for addressing local and global challenges to the Jewish people.*

But there is substantial resentment and backlash developing in Israel and the United States. Eventually, as happened in the last half of the first millennium, the rejected and disenfranchised Jews will gradually reduce their support of Orthodox Jewry and the Ultra Orthodox community will slip into abject poverty exactly as it did in the sixth century. And those disenfranchised Jews who had formerly provided sustenance to

---

109 The three major population groups are: Reform. 41.4%, Conservative. 40.4%, Orthodox. 6.8%.

110 Because of their implied engagement with the Gentile community, this obviously refers only to the non-ultra-orthodox Jews.

the ultra orthodox community will move on, seeking new opportunities, new comforts, new affiliations, and new inspirations.

The NJPS goes on to point out that

> Migration and mobility also characterize the Jewish population. Over time, many native-born Jews have migrated from the Northeast and Midwest to the South and West. In addition, more than one-third of adult Jews lived in a different residence five years ago than they do today. Migration and mobility have important implications for the communal system. Residential movement may disrupt established communal connections, and forging connections in new locations may take a sustained period of time[111].

And in the concluding paragraph of the NJPS report, the crux of the matter:

> In sum, contrasting trends in Jewish involvement, the sharp differentiation between affiliated and unaffiliated Jews, and significant differences between the in-married and intermarried all suggest an increasing polarization in Jewish connections. Over time, some segments of the American Jewish population evince greater involvement in Jewish life, while other segments show signs of disengagement. Indeed, this apparent pattern encompasses strength, challenge, and diversity, the very themes of this report, and will likely serve as the basis of important policy discussions in the American Jewish community.

THE TRUE JEW

Our granddaughter Isabel mentioned at dinner one night that she was the only "True Jew" in her class. She lives with her parents in a relatively Jewish suburban community that boasts three synagogues. She explained that by "True Jew" she meant that she was the only Jewish child in her Public School class who has two born-Jewish parents. "Surely, that must be different in Hebrew school," I asked. "Yes," she replied, "There are a few other 'True Jews' in Hebrew School, but most are not."

There actually are quite a few Jewish students in Isabel's class. But their parents are not high visibility Jews and it would be impossible to identify them as Jews. They self identify as Jewish and their children are Jewish. Some of them are passive synagogue members, some go to services only on the holidays, some light candles on Chanukah, some attend a Seder and eat matzo on Passover; some light candles on Friday night, some keep kosher, some don't. They celebrate happy occasions in the

---

111 From The National Jewish Population Study of 2000–2001.

Jewish tradition and they mourn their parents in the Jewish manner. And they laugh familiarly at "Jewish Jokes".

The unique factor about these children that Isabel described is that they are not unique. They, in Isabel's case, are children of Jewish middle class suburban parents, but they could be in any class and in any place. They, and their parents are, in fact, the True Jews because they have made a conscious effort to live as Jews and to raise their children with the understanding and pride of being Jewish. They could have chosen otherwise. There was no pressure on them; no rabbinic dictum; no threat of exclusion or excommunication, and no threat of punishment nor promise of reward. There was just the satisfaction of being associated with, and teaching their children about, the Jewish heritage, promise and obligations.

But without a new Jewish revival that invigorates Judaism, these True Jews will eventually return to the shadows from which their eighteenth century ancestors emerged.

In that century the spirituality of the Hasidim[112] joined with the social consciousness of the Mussar movement, and the intellectual stimulation of the Haskalah to create a unique environment that reinvigorated Judaism. These three movements, along with the introduction of Reform and Conservative Judaism, opened the door to the unaffiliated and disenfranchised and enthusiastically welcomed them back into Judaism. Although initially the traditional rabbis opposed each of these movements, when they saw the numbers of Jews that had surfaced and rejoined the religion they ended their opposition and even absorbed, adapted, and co-opted many of the aspects of these new movements. It was the return and revival of the formerly uncounted unaffiliated "missing" Jews that reinvigorated Judaism and saved the day. The recorded number of Jews in the world nearly quadrupled in the hundred years from 1840 to 1940[113]. The rate of Jewish population growth was twice the world population growth rate[114].

---

112 Specifically, the Hasidism as presented by the Baal Shem Tov.
113 The population grew from 4,600,000 to 16,700,000.
114 This is all the more remarkable when you consider that the world population growth rate included the population explosion in third world countries.

But the world is a different place today. Hasidism has become just another name for ultra orthodox, and the Haskalah and Mussar movements have been absorbed into the basic fiber of liberal Judaism. The Conservative and Reform movements have lost their luster and they now struggle for relevance; and the more they struggle, the more irrelevant they become. The old "new" rules no longer apply and the old "old" rules are stale. Judaism has become a shell filled with poseurs, pontificators, and prognosticators, without a visionary among them. The giant prophets like the Baal Shem Tov, Israel Salanter, and Moses Mendelssohn who courageously brought fresh thinking and a new path to Judaism in the last century do not have modern successors and their impact has faded.

What remains is a proud and profound Jewish heritage. "Fine tuning" no longer matters, and repackaging doesn't work. "Great new ideas to save the Jewish people" have come and gone like tumbleweed in the desert, and with every new repackaging the great majority of Jews become more disenchanted and fade away at an ever accelerating rate.

The late eighteenth century was a time of great world-wide awakening. Open communication and the sharing of ideas and inspirations became readily available. The Jew, who had been demonized for nearly two millennia, was now able to communicate with the non-Jew on a nearly level field. In a very brief time the Jews moved from darkness into light, from isolation to inclusion, from a self imposed insulation to nearly complete integration, from separation to assimilation.

And this assimilation benefited Jews in every walk of life and in every religious affiliation. Every Jewish denomination grew in numbers, influence and affluence. Jews of all beliefs and affiliations were integrated into nearly every aspect of Western society.

Today, like the late eighteenth century, there is a new opportunity for Judaism. The internet and its leveling social media have created an opportunity for the True Jews to communicate with each other in an open forum and on a level playing field. Websites like Jdate, Facebook, and Linkedin Groups effortlessly unite disparate Jewish individuals and communities, while trendy on line Jewish newspapers like Tablet provide Jewish news in a breezy twenty-first century style. Discussion forums exist on virtually every Jewish topic; and blogs give individual Jews an opportunity to express and discuss specifically Jewish thoughts and feelings.

The True Jew struggles every day to make his Judaism meaningful. The True Jew may light candles on Friday night because she believes that this is her personal time to express her most innermost wishes. The True Jew appreciates the value of the Sabbath as an oasis at the end of the week — a relief from the pressures of her job — an occasion to spend time with her family and enjoy the luxuries that she has accumulated — not as a prohibition against turning on lights. The true Jew appreciates the period of introspection and mutual forgiveness that is the basis of the Rosh Hashanah and Yom Kippur holidays. The True Jew is active socially for the betterment of his community and fellow man. The True Jew celebrates the historic achievements of his ancestors. The True Jew can laugh at himself. And the True Jew struggles every day to pass these values and morals and fiber on to his[115] children.

The True Jew lives in the modern world; challenged by the same issues as his Gentile neighbors. The True Jew learns to accept and welcome his non-Jewish daughter-in-law or son-in-law. The True Jew patiently tells his child and his grand child and his great-grandchild how fortunate they are to have been born into Judaism's wonderful tradition of familial love and social responsibility. The True Jew is generous with her time and her fortune[116] to help whatever causes she chooses to support, Jewish or otherwise.

The True Jew might be inspired by a moving sermon, or an emotional cantor, or a beautiful sanctuary, or an act of charity and kindness, or an act of generosity, or a beautiful painting, or a musical performance. God is present in all of these in equal measure.

The True Jew might attend weekly synagogue services or once a year or never at all. But as long as he affirms that he is a Jew, he is a Jew — a True Jew. Though he may be indistinguishable from his Gentile neighbors, the True Jew nevertheless maintains his pride in being Jewish and his commitment to Jewish continuity.

---

115 I have tried to maintain gender neutrality in my description of the True Jew, but for expedience's sake, I have used male pronouns.

116 According to the Pew Forum, 46% of the Jewish population of the US earns over $100,000. This is the highest percentage of any major religious group.

But the Haredi rabbinic Jewish community is attempting to shift the Jewish center of gravity. They are trying to make Judaism a graded institution in which the ultra orthodox are assigning the grades (A+ for ultra Orthodox, B for Conservative, C for Reconstructionist, D for Reform, F for unaffiliated). They would like today's Jews to rate themselves and each other by the level of their religious dedication. They would like the assimilated Jew to refer to himself as "not a very 'good' Jew". But they are wrong. *There is no gradation of Jews. You either are a Jew or not — there are no shades of grey*[117]. As Andre Sassoon, vice president of the International Jewish Committee, Sefarad '92 said as he welcomed the participation of the Southwest Secret Jews[118]: "We [Jews] are a tolerant people. Personally, whether someone is truly a Jew or not, only God can judge, and not mortals."

True Jews, Jews who love their religion and respect its values and continuity must not allow rabbinic Jewry to once again establish exclusionary criteria as they did, with such harmful effect, in the first five hundred years of the Common Era.

It is time for the True Jews to take back their religion. Sure, there is room for the ultra orthodox but they and their religious values are no more authentic than those of any other Jews — including fully assimilated Jews. If the ultra orthodox choose to wear eighteenth century dress and side curls and wigs, that's their prerogative but it is not, by any measure, either authentic Jewish clothing or authentic Jewish behavior. In fact, it is easy to be an ultra orthodox Jew. All you have to do is suppress your ego and subjugate yourself to the whims and rulings of the "Rebbe." It's much more difficult to be a True Jew[119].

In the next few chapters I will outline a possibly shocking suggestion for the form that the new Judaism should adopt. Just as the rabbinic Jews of the early eighteenth century could not possibly have anticipated the growth, strength, and diversification of the Jewish community that

---

117 The Nazis did not consider synagogue participation when they marched the Jews to their death.

118 These are the Jews of Spain who fled to Mexico at the time of the Inquisition and were forced to convert to Christianity but retained some secret vestiges of their Jewish identity.

119 My grandfather used to say, "Zeyr shvehr tzu zein a Yid" — "It's so difficult to be a Jew."

occurred in the following two hundred years, the True Jew of the twenty-first century must be open to new ideas and opportunities.

The True Jews must not be willing to wait for the "stars" to be in the right order for another revival of Judaism. They must not seek a sign from the heavens nor a charismatic "messianic" leader on earth. They must stand proudly at the front of their religion, welcoming and being welcomed at the same time. They must set no barriers to being Jewish, no entry requirements, and no limitations. They must declare, "Now is the time for the "True Jew" to once again lead his people into the light."

To our granddaughter Isabel I say, yes, she is a True Jew, but so are the others. And she and they are the hope and future of the Jewish people.

To Infinity and Beyond: What If...[120]

Suppose there were no synagogues. Where would you pray? The simple answer is that you would pray privately at home, after all, Judaism is essentially a personal religion. But there are certain occasions when you need a minyan (a quorum of 10 people) like when you say mourner's Kaddish.

So, if you needed to say mourner's Kaddish, you would call up some of your Jewish friends and ask them to stop by your house for a few minutes so that you could say the necessary prayers with the necessary minyan.

But then, what about Shabbat? Don't you need a quorum for some of the prayers?

That gets a little more complicated. You'd have to invite some friends to come to your house on Friday night and again on Saturday morning and possibly once again on Saturday evening so that you could all say your prayers together.

You'd probably have to add some inducement to get them to keep coming every Shabbat. Maybe you'd serve bagels & lox after services, maybe you'd invite someone to facilitate a discussion, or maybe you'd invite someone to teach some songs.

Maybe you would join forces with someone else who needs or wants a minyan, but it's certain that you would have to do something to keep your friends coming back every week. Eventually, if everything works

---

120 This is attributed to Buzz Lightyear.

out, some sort of camaraderie would evolve, and the friends might share the hosting responsibilities.

As the involvement grows, you might also seek out someone who knows more about Judaism to guide your little group — a teacher or a singer — a rabbinic student — maybe a recent graduate — maybe a cantorial student — someone with Judaic knowledge and some social skills. You'd have to pay him something — at least his expenses — and maybe some sort of compensation to induce him to spend time during the week preparing the class that he'll teach on Shabbat.

It probably would also make sense to create some sort of fund to reimburse the host for the lox and bagels — so you all chip in a few bucks and you open a bank account.

The trouble is, it's becoming a bit of a burden for everyone — having to show up every weekend, having to support the teacher, and having to pay for the food.

So you all get together and decide to widen the base. You'll each invite two couples to join the group. That way, instead of ten people you'll have thirty people — 15 couples[121].

Now suppose the student rabbi that you've hired wants to increase his income and really do a good job every week. He figures that he would like to make $20,000 a year. That works out to nearly $700 a person!

You tell him that you just don't love being Jewish that much and besides you've got a lot of other expenses. But he's a good leader and you don't want to lose him. Plus, he can teach your children to read the Torah for their bar mitzvah, and maybe also, he has been visiting your mom in a nursing home on the way to your house.

So he says, "How much can you afford?"

You say, not more that $250 a person — $500 a family a year — that would work out to $10 per family per week.

So he says OK but at $500 a family you'd have to add at least twenty-five more families. That would make a total of forty families.

"But that's almost a hundred people! We can't fit them into anyone's house!"

---

121 This is how the synagogue that my wife and I founded over thirty years ago started.

"First of all," he says, "not all of them will come at any one time unless it's a special occasion. Second, with a hundred people you'll be able to share the responsibilities."

"But what about special occasions when everyone will want to come and even bring guests?"

"Then you'll have to rent space," he says. "But only for those special occasions, and you probably could either all chip in for the rent or ask the family that's making the special celebration to pay for the space."

"Where could we get space like that to use only a few times a year?"

"Well, there's the Women's Club, and the V.F.W. hall for starters. You could get a local florist to decorate it and I have an armoire that will make a perfect ark for the Torah. Lots of synagogues, by the way, have extra torahs that they'd be happy to lend you."

"It sounds good to me," you say.

"Not so fast," says he. "There's one more thing — and it's a tough call. I'm a student right now. I take classes all week and I work here on the weekend. First of all, I'll be graduating this year. Second, I want to be a full time rabbi with a congregation of my own. And I want to be *your* rabbi."

"But we can't afford a full-time rabbi!" you gasp.

"No you can't, at least not with only forty families. But what if you had a hundred families, each paying $500 per year? That would yield $50,000; allow $10,000 for expenses and that would leave me an income of $40,000."

"Can you live on $40,000?"

"No, I can't; at least not for the long run. I'd have to find ways of augmenting my income. I could do tutoring, for example. Instead of sending your kids to Hebrew School, I would tutor the older ones on a one-to-one basis and tutor the younger ones in groups. After all, with a hundred families there will probably be about twenty kids who are pre bar mitzvah.

"Let's say I charge $500 for each of the kids who are in the last year before their Bar Mitzvahs, and $200 for each of the other kids. That's about another $7,000."

"That all sounds good," you say, "but can you live on $47,000?"

"Not for long."

"So what will you do?"

"I will do what every successful businessman does," he says. "I will expand the base. As long as I am offering a good product at a reasonable cost people will flock to our group. Instead of a hundred families, we might have three hundred families, and instead of $47,000 I would be earning over a hundred thousand. Plus, I'll have money left over to hire some staff and rent a place full time."

"Hey," you counter, "this is starting to sound like a regular shul."

"Yes, it is. Except with one major difference: It is going to be self-sustaining and I will run it on a fee for services basis......"

"What does that mean?"

"Well, first of all it means that the $500 per family that you pay will cover the basic synagogue services — prayer services every Friday night, Saturday morning and Saturday evening and everything that goes with them like a sermon, torah reading and discussion; just like we've been having. It will cover all major holiday services as well. In fact, it will cover everything that a typical synagogue offers, and of course I'll always be available for pastoral care like visits to the sick. But it will not cover any classes, or weddings, or funerals, or any spiritual guidance sessions. It will not cover my income from speaking engagements, or income from my book, or advertising in the synagogue newsletter, or anything that is outside of the synagogue. I will write up a schedule listing the services that are included in membership and a schedule of prices for those services that are not included."

"That sounds fair, but where do you think you will get two hundred more families from?"

"That is my challenge. This is a fairly Jewish community, but only about 40% of the families are affiliated with a synagogue. That means about six hundred Jewish families are not affiliated with a synagogue. For some it's a matter of philosophy, for some it's a matter of expense, for others it's because no one asked them. I plan to ask them.

"Most synagogues charge around $1500 for membership plus a building fund contribution, plus Hebrew School. When they discover how inexpensive it is to belong to our synagogue, and how accessible I am, and how eager I am for them to join, they will join in droves. Did you know that nearly 100% of Jews have belonged to a synagogue at some point in their lives?

"Most of them leave — unhappily — because the synagogue was too expensive, or didn't meet their needs, or they didn't like the rabbi, or who knows why — it's like any other business — you have to satisfy the customers."

"Wait!" you exclaim, "what about your board? They'll never approve anything like this!"

"What board?" he replies. "This is a self sustaining private enterprise. It will sink or swim on the strength of what I do. That's the beauty of it. The pressure is constantly on me to keep my product as desirable as possible so that I can attract as many customers as possible.

"But there is one pressure which I will have to keep my eye on — competition. If I'm as successful in this community as I think I will be, then other rabbis will come in and open their own shuls. I can't be all things to all people — other denominations will get into the game, other rabbis will try to lure away parts of my congregation.

"That's called competition. And competition is good. It's what built America and it can revive Judaism."

"That's an interesting concept you've developed," you say. "What do you call it?"

"I call it the entrepreneurial rabbi and the self-sustaining synagogue."

THE GREAT RABBIS OF YORE

Throughout Jewish history since the destruction of the Temple and the subsequent Diaspora, rabbis have primarily been looked upon as teachers — sources of information — and the final arbiters of all things Jewish. In fact, the word rabbi implies teacher, and the Yiddish word for synagogue, shul, literally means school. Some early synagogues even retain the name "Bais Hamedrash" which means house of study. In the nineteenth century, mostly through the rise of Reform Judaism, rabbis and cantors took on the additional, highly visible role as orators and entertainers. Great synagogues were built on the strength of the drawing power of a particular rabbi or cantor. Attending services was a combina-tion of prayer, social exposure, education, and entertainment.

Even today, older people speak of the golden days of the great rab-bis of old — Joachim Prinz, Stephen Wise, Abraham Joshua Heschel, and Joseph Soloveitchik, to name a few, and the great cantors — Moshe Kusevitsky, Gershon Sirota, Moishe Oysher, and Josef Rosenblatt — of their youth. Even today, cantors and rabbis, and the stimulation and en-tertainment that they provide are a major factor in the life and attractive-ness of many prominent synagogues. For example, cantor Yitzchok Meir Helfgot, the cantor of Park East Synagogue in New York, receives a salary above $300,000 which is more than the entire budget of many smaller synagogues, and members of the choir are paid on a scale not unlike the chorus at the Metropolitan Opera.

Rabbis and cantors are often paid in excess of $150,000 plus such perks as parsonage allowances, trips to Israel, sabbatical years, and sum-mer-long vacations.

Many of the nation's largest synagogues consider the investment in the drawing power of rabbis and cantors to be worthwhile, and they point to the sharp drop in attendance when neither the primary rabbi nor the cantor is performing.

But, with the advent of alternative and affordable forms of entertain-ment, the draw of these performers of religious ritual has diminished. Most Jews join synagogues, not to be wowed by the entertainment, but to fulfill their religious obligations. The fact that 61% of synagogue mem-bers are younger than fifty five seems to indicate that most of these Jews have joined the synagogue to fulfill their obligation to bring their chil-dren to bar mitzvah. Once that obligation has been fulfilled, they drift away from the synagogues in overwhelming numbers.

For centuries rabbis have been the arbiters of Jewish law (Halachah). Worshipers and members of their community came to them for advice on kosher foods, ritual observance, family relationships, and issues of ethics. But today, a simple Google search will yield pronouncements by highly regarded (and some less highly regarded) authorities on just about any-thing Jewish, and on virtually any aspect of Judaism. (A search under "kosher chicken," for example, yielded 7,660,000 results; "Jewish inter-marriage" yielded 770,000.)

Some rabbis, especially orthodox ones, have become providers of timely advice. They have made themselves available to the community 24/7 and they are often called upon to give rulings on kashruth, to help with marital problems[122], to offer financial advice, and to be an under-standing and sympathetic "ear." Their wives are also expected to be avail-able to the community for consultation and consolation. In the Conser-vative and Reform communities, the rabbi is expected to be the public face of the community and to appear and represent the congregation at all public functions. Members of congregations have been known to comment on their rabbi's weight, grooming, choice of clothing, and espe-cially his wife's modesty and style. The behavior of their children might also come under critical scrutiny.

Most rabbis, unfortunately, have been relegated to the role of per-formers. They perform circumcisions, they perform bar mitzvahs, they perform weddings, and they perform funerals. Their other function, that of spiritual leader, is often nothing more than a combination of sermon giver and cheerleader. People often join a synagogue because they "like" the rabbi; and they leave just as often because they don't "like" the new rabbi.

So what's a rabbi to do? They have attended rabbinic school for at least four years, and have spent thousands of hours in study. They have been exposed to the greatest rabbinic minds of this and previous cen-turies. They have studied both highly relevant and obscure tractates, learned how to read and speak Hebrew, learned how to chant all the various Torah and megillot trope, they have studied in Israel, they have been camp councilors, they have learned "clinical pastoral education," they have committed themselves to "a lifetime of service to God, the Jew-ish community, and all of humanity",[123] and they're often being judged, even in the most orthodox communities, on the most superficial aspects of their lives.

---

122 One rabbi I know received a phone call from a groom on his wedding night asking for advice because his bride had barricaded herself in the bathroom.
123 This is quoted from the Jewish Theological Seminary's website.

They have learned how to be scholars, but they haven't learned how to be rabbis. They haven't learned how to make a living, or manage their household finances, or even negotiate a contract. They haven't learned how to build a congregation, or even how to satisfy a congregation. They haven't learned how to function in the twenty-first century; in fact, they haven't learned one thing that is different from what they would have learned in a rabbinic seminary a hundred or more years ago. They have spent nearly $200,000 on their education, and they will never use most of the things they learned.

Here, for example, is a list of the courses offered at the New York campus of Hebrew Union College, the college for Reform rabbis:

Bible & its interpretation

Communal Service

Doctor of Ministry

Education

History

Jewish Language & Literature

Music

Professional Development

Rabbinics

Religious Thought and Ethics Education

Talmud

Thesis Requirements

Worship and Ritual

The only one of these subjects that implies twenty-first century skills is "Professional Development." The following is a list of the topics included under Professional Development:

Clergy Counseling for the Life Cycle

Advanced Speech

Life Cycle Music for the Rabbi

Tough Choices: Major Social Issues and Opportunities for Change[124]

---

124 This course discusses "effective and courageous leadership skills through which we can heal and strengthen society."

Synagogue 2000: Spiritual Leadership for Synagogues: Theory and Application[125]

Independent Study: Spiritual Guidance

Hospital Chaplaincy

None of these subjects covers the twenty-first century skills necessary for today's rabbis.

Sure, the new rabbis know how to read the Torah, but most large synagogues have a regular Torah reader and a cantor. Sure, they know all the intricacies of Halachah, but they will rarely or never be called upon to express them. Sure, they know the Talmudic sources, but the discussions that they found so stimulating in rabbinic school will rarely see the light of day in their synagogue. Sure, they have been taught how to "heal and strengthen society," but they will most likely never have the opportunity to implement these skills; and sure, they have been given a "spiritual vision with insights into organizational development," but they haven't learned the how-to of writing a mission or vision statement, or a strategic plan.

They will discover that their synagogue sermons must be simple and accessible to the masses — and that means *all* the masses, not just the intellectuals. They will learn to answer questions simply and directly without referring to the historic scholarship that they have acquired. They will learn that sitting with a child and making a shofar out of paper is valued even more highly than the writing of an erudite treatise on Tanach and they will learn that how they dress and how they shake hands has a greater impact on their future than their fluency in Hebrew.

Most mainstream rabbis are simply not prepared to be rabbis. They are prepared to be scholars, they are prepared to be "guardians of the faith," but they are not prepared to be successful rabbis. In fact, they are prepared for almost certain failure.

---

125 This course offers "a blend of spiritual vision with insights into organizational development, translated into a conceptual framework drawn from Jewish tradition."

The Rewards of Academic Success

There is a complex obstacle course that rabbis must negotiate between a student's academic success and the synagogue marketplace.

The first obstacle is the extremely harmful double standard for measuring rabbinic success. In school, the criterion for measuring success is academic, which is relatively easy to measure on the basis of grades. This is the part of the traditional report card which is above the line and is based on absolute academic scores. But in the synagogue marketplace, the measure is social success. This is the part of the traditional report card that is below the line and includes judgments about behavior such as "gets along well with others." This criterion is often much more crucial to the success of the rabbi, and is much more difficult to measure. These two criteria are often mutually exclusive. The more socially skilled student does not always have the highest academic skills, nor does the trouble-maker have the worst.

The greatest hurdle and by far the most complex, is the placement service. In the Conservative Movement[126] for example, the Joint Placement Commission of the Rabbinical Assembly (RA) acts as a filter between synagogues and rabbis. This commission selects candidates from its 1,648 members to fill vacant positions in synagogues. Every graduate of a rabbinical school that is certified by the Rabbinical Assembly automatically becomes a member of the Rabbinical Assembly and thus is subject to their placement procedures. Essentially, the way this placement service works at its simplest, is that the synagogue notifies the RA that they expect to have a vacancy. The RA then chooses a few candidates and forwards their resumes to the synagogue. The synagogue then schedules interviews and try-outs with the best of these candidates[127].

The synagogue and the candidate are prohibited from having direct contact with one another unless they go through the RA. Thus, if a synagogue knows of a rabbinical student or a rabbi who has the unique skills that they require, they are not allowed to contact that rabbi directly. Conversely, if a rabbi hears of a synagogue that has potential that he feels

---

126 There are similar placement services for the Reform and Orthodox movements.

127 At the time that I am writing there are many more candidates than positions.

he can build on; he is precluded from contacting that synagogue directly. In practice this creates some very disappointing results. A promising rabbi with a vision cannot search out to a congregation in which he can fulfill his vision nor can a congregation with a specific need recruit a fitting candidate.

According to its website, the RA's mission is to assist unhappy congregations and rabbis to work things out. Only as a last resort will they consider replacing a sitting rabbi, and they will rarely consider allowing a rabbi to move from one congregation to another without going through them. Their intention, it seems, is to level the playing field as much as possible by sending the strongest candidates to needy synagogues and the relatively weaker candidates to the strongest synagogues.

Gerald Zelizer, a former president of the Rabbinical Assembly, recounts the story of Rabbi Howard Handler who "alleged that his congregation in Manhattan had not renewed his contract after learning through an anonymous phone call that he was gay and that he sought rabbinical placement[128] in another Synagogue." Rabbi Zelizer recounts how he attempted to fashion a compromise:

> My vice president and I crafted a compromise proposal which we felt would treat our colleague compassionately, yet at the same time maintain heterosexuality as the religious norm. Would the Placement Commission agree to allow Rabbi Handler to seek placement on his own initiative, without penalty, within the Conservative movement? My argument had been that this compromise enabled us to "grandfather" an already existent member, without abrogating the movement's policy not to ordain a law or accept homosexual rabbis into the RA. This item was put on the agenda of the Executive Council meeting of June 1994. On the eve of that meeting, I was heartened that both the Seminary and United Synagogue representatives on the Placement Commission agreed to the compromise. Seventy communications from RA members objecting to our treatment of Rabbi Handler underscored both the public and volatile nature of this dispute.

> To my consternation, the Joint Placement Commission rejected the compromise; instead they ruled that Rabbi Handler could not be placed at that time. In their view, he had violated the halakhah [religious laws] of the movement as clearly as if had violated the Shabbat. Frustrated that a solu-

---

128 The quote is from the article: "Members of the RA may find employment only through the aegis of the movement's Joint Placement Commission, based on a system of seniority and eligibility. Neither rabbis nor congregations can arrange work outside of this system."

tion had slipped through my fingers, I reacted indignantly to the chairman, and in our teleconference call communicated my disappointment to the Executive Council. The council, agitated that we could not find relief for our colleague, instructed our professional staff not to penalize him if he sought a position on his own initiative. It allowed him to be the exception to the general rule that members of the RA can find congregational employment only through the aegis of the movement's joint Placement Commission.[129]

Thus, when a large, financially viable synagogue is looking for an assistant rabbi, the candidates that they get to interview probably might not be the best and the brightest, but rather the ones that the RA feels, for various reasons, would be the best fit. As can be seen from the above, there are many considerations that go into the matchmaking process and academic success and personality are only two of the factors. In practice the "straight A" graduates who might be considered the most desirable are often not sent to the largest synagogues.

For the most part, these large synagogues have achieved their success on the shoulders of a charismatic rabbi. They are seeking another "star" to become assistant rabbi to the "chief" rabbi. They hope that the current rabbi and administration can take advantage of the new assistant rabbi's natural skills and seamlessly integrate the new rabbi into the synagogue structure.

In practice, the assistant rabbi that they are sent is usually not the best and brightest. He is relegated to auxiliary responsibilities like bar mitzvah training and assisting in the Hebrew school. On rare occasions, he might be allowed to conduct a secondary service, and perhaps even deliver a sermon. His pastoral duties might also include visiting the sick (but not the really important members).

But unlike rookie baseball players in the minor leagues who hope that they will have an opportunity to demonstrate their worth so that they will be "traded" to a "triple A" farm team and eventually into the major leagues, these assistant rabbis never get an opportunity to shine. Eventually they are replaced by another mid range assistant rabbi and they move on to become the rabbi of a small synagogue where, even though they may have obvious skills, they might languish for years.

---

129 Copyright 1995 American Jewish Congress.

For the most part, these small synagogues are struggling for a variety of reasons, and the new young rabbi is ill equipped to deal with their problems. The Peter Principle[130] immediately takes effect and the synagogue and the new rabbi are forced to make adjustments downward.

Of course there are exceptions to this pattern, but the system is structured to achieve failure and sadly, it is usually successful.

The superior graduates, on the other hand, are sent to small and mid-size synagogues where there is perceived potential for growth. These young rabbis are thrust immediately into leadership roles and are expected excite the membership and help it grow into a larger, more successful synagogue. Often, however, because they have not had an apprenticeship or sufficiently thorough experience, these young rabbis are not ready for "prime time" and they too fail.

When they are successful at this effort they are considered super stars and they and the synagogue grows. But if they should falter, then they are branded as disappointments; the synagogues seek their replacement, and they are relegated to secondary positions.

Because of the RA's filtering process, the options of these stumbling rabbis are limited. They must go where the RA sends them and they are precluded from seeking employment in another synagogue without the RA's imprimatur. This is the exact opposite of a meritocracy. The high scoring students end up in small to middle range, often struggling synagogues where they must sink or swim without the momentum of a large synagogue, while the mid range students end up with the credentials and experience of having been apprentice to a "star" rabbi at a major institution.

This leads to an interesting and possibly fatal imbalance. The large synagogues who built their membership on the strength of a charismatic rabbi are given a weaker rabbi as his eventual replacement. But

---

130 The Peter Principle, which was formulated by Dr. Laurence J. Peter and Raymond Hull, states that "in a hierarchy every employee tends to rise to his level of incompetence", meaning that employees tend to be promoted until they reach a position at which they cannot work competently. The principle holds that in a hierarchy, members are promoted so long as they work competently. Eventually they are promoted to a position at which they are no longer competent, and there they remain, being unable to earn further promotions.

their membership and their physical plant had grown because of the attractiveness and skills of their senior rabbi. And now, with a new, lesser rabbi, their membership slowly begins to fade away and the maintenance of their plant becomes an increasing burden on the remaining congregants[131]. On the other hand, the small synagogue that has just hired the most promising young rabbi begins to grow and rapidly outgrows its facilities. They build a new, larger synagogue and they continue to grow and add services and members. But eventually, their rabbi ages and the same leveling processes begin again.

Thus, the rewards of scholastic success may be opposite from normal expectations. A brilliant scholar is forced to struggle with frustration, while his mediocre classmate is doomed to failure having been given an opportunity that he cannot fulfill.

The placement division of the Orthodox Union, the Rabbinical Council of America (RCA) has policies similar to the Conservative movement. As its on line membership benefits summary states:

> The Joint Placement Committee of the RCA, The Orthodox Union, and Yeshiva University (and staffed by the latter) is the major placement service bringing together Orthodox synagogues and Orthodox rabbis, to respond to and fill their mutual need for effective rabbinic leadership. Synagogues and communities around the world turn to this committee to assist them in filling all kinds of rabbinic positions on various levels. To be considered for placement by the committee, a rabbi must first be (or be about to become) a member in good standing of the RCA (unless he is a musmach of RIETS already).

> Similarly, Orthodox rabbis who wish to be considered for military chaplaincy positions must be sponsored by a rabbinic agency, and the RCA fulfills that role for its members, as a Sponsoring Organization for chaplaincy affairs recognized by the US Armed Forces.

> The RCA provides support, guidance, and, where requested, intercession, on behalf of its members involved in contract negotiations, lay-rabbinic relationships, and associated support services. These services are provided by the RCA via the Director of Rabbinic Services.

The placement arm of the Union for Reform Judaism however, has a different, less ideologically driven initial placement program. They invite members of interested congregations to interview the graduates. Then through a double blind procedure, both the candidates and the syna-

---

131   And this accelerates the rate of departure.

gogues prioritize their selections. A committee then reviews these selections and makes its recommendations.

Once the students are initially placed in synagogues however, the
process becomes similar to the RA in that neither the synagogues nor
their rabbis can make a move without the input and approval of the
placement arm of the Union for Reform Judaism.

There Are Rabbis and There Are Rabbis

The imbalance in Judaism is remarkable. There can be two synagogues in the same town serving the same Jewish population. One might
be phenomenally successful and the other might be just hanging on. The
weaker one looks enviously at the more successful one. They think —
"that synagogue is more traditional — maybe we should become more
traditional." Or they think — "that synagogue is more liberal — maybe
we should be more liberal." Or they think that synagogue has music Friday night, or that synagogue has a more beautiful building, or that synagogue does catering or is more politically active or whatever. You get the
point — they are jealous and they can't figure out what they need to do
to catch up, so they focus on the "sizzle" rather than the steak.

This reminds me of the old joke about three owners of a dying movie
theater. The first says that they need to put velvet on their seats; the second says that they need to put chintz on their seats. The third says, "We
don't need velvet and we don't need chintz. What we need on the seats
is tuchases [butts]."

The point is that the success or failure of a synagogue depends upon
a variety of factors. But the most overarching factor is the personality of
the rabbi. A rabbi can make or break a synagogue. Charisma, while hard
to nail down, clearly has an enormous impact. And that impact, though
it usually originates from the rabbi, pervades all aspects of the congregation. There is a clearly perceptible energy that successful synagogues
exude. Potential congregants are drawn to it and current congregants
smugly boast about it. The prayers are the same, the ritual is the same,
the same things are being taught in the Hebrew School, the physical
plant is equivalent, yet there is something intangible that one synagogue
has that another doesn't.

Sometimes the super synagogue buys its stars, like the Park East Synagogue in New York. But the cost of those stars is prohibitive and only the wealthiest of synagogues can afford superstars. More often, the successful synagogue has a rabbi who has grown with the synagogue. His energy, charm and intelligence are contagious. This rabbi often seems ubiquitous. He is working with the children in the pre-school program and he is doing study groups with the seniors. He directs the synagogue library growth plan, sits on the town advisory board and oversees holiday festival plans, and still has time to meet with individual families. Plus, he delivers wonderful sermons, leads interesting discussions, and knows all of the members of the synagogue by their first names. He has a pleasant word for everyone he meets, whether at services or in the local super market.

He is, for want of a better word, a superstar. And people gravitate to him the same way that people gravitate to any charismatic person. That's what charisma is and as the saying goes, some people got it and some people don't. But superstars are not born. Sure they are unique but they still put their pants on one leg at a time. They still have issues with their families, and they still have personal shortcomings just like everyone else. But there's something about them that makes them popular — that makes people want to be with them and do things with them.

Every synagogue is on the lookout for these super star rabbis and every synagogue wants to hire them. But sometimes, when the potential super stars join a synagogue their remarkable people-skills fade away. Sometimes the synagogue, though it tries to be receptive to the new rabbi's powerful personality, pushes back against him. This often happens in a synagogue that is supported by a small clique of wealthy donors, or a coterie of founders and old-timers who resist change.

These old-timers *say* that they would like new blood and that they like the way the new rabbi reaches out to the community, but they really *don't* like it. And that's because they are afraid of losing power — losing control. They love their synagogue just as it is; and they're not about to stand by and watch the newcomers dilute and destroy what they have come to believe is "their" synagogue.

Modern Jewish history is full of stories of once thriving synagogues that can no longer survive even though they are in heavily Jewish areas. Some apologists point to the youth or lack of commitment of the Jews in the area. Others point to the age of the community, and that many of the potential members are snowbirds who spend their winters in Florida. Still others blame nearby shopping malls, and other diversions like soccer, lacrosse, field hockey, and football practice. "What's a synagogue to do when there are so many other things going on," they whine.

Yet down the block, or in the next town, there's a synagogue that's thriving.

A typical example of the impact of a rabbi and cantor can be seen in the recent history of Bnai Jeshurun, one of the most well attended synagogues in New York City.

Founded in 1825, Bnai Jeshurun was the second synagogue founded in New York, and the third oldest Ashkenazi synagogue in the United States. It was founded by a coalition of young members of congregation Shearith Israel and immigrants and the descendants of immigrants from the Germany and Poland. The first rabbi, Samuel Isaacs, was appointed in 1839. By 1850, the congregation had grown large enough to make it necessary to build a new synagogue on Green Street.

In 1865, the congregation moved yet again, to a new building on 34th Street, part of the site of the flagship Macy's store. Driven by the rapid expansion of the city, and their own growth and confidence they moved yet again in 1885 to Madison Avenue at 65th Street and again in 1917 to the present building on West 88th Street between Broadway and West End Avenue.

But times changed, their faithful membership aged and moved away and a new younger "yuppy" population had started moving into the neighborhood. These new young Jews were seemingly not interested in synagogue membership. By the early 1980s, this proud synagogue, which had a glorious sanctuary, an impressive building, and a separate Hebrew School building reached its low point of just 40 remaining families. They sold their religious school building, and were teetering on the brink of extinction, with serious financial woes and difficulty attracting a minyan.

But then, in August 1985, Rabbi Marshall T. Meyer, a noted charismatic spiritual leader and human rights champion, was installed as spiritual leader. Rabbi Meyer was an American-born Conservative rabbi, and a recognized international human rights activist who had never had experience as a pulpit rabbi in the United States.

He was born in New York City, attended Dartmouth College, and was ordained by the Rabbinical School at the Jewish Theological Seminary in 1958. Upon his ordination, he took a position outside the United States as Assistant Rabbi at the Congregación Israelita de la República Argentina in Buenos Aires, Argentina. His charismatic character turned him immediately into an important figure in the Argentine Jewish community. He founded the Seminario Rabínico Latinoamericano, where dozens of Spanish-speaking rabbis who would serve communities in Argentina, Latin America and the rest of the world were ordained.

Rabbi Meyer also founded and led Comunidad Bet El, a congregation that became a model that many other Conservative synagogues in Argentina and Latin America emulated.

During the years of the Argentine military regime of 1976–1982, Rabbi Meyer became a strong critic of the military government and its violations of human rights. In 1983, when democracy was reestablished in Argentina, Rabbi Meyer returned to the United States and, after a short stay on the faculty of the University of Judaism in Los Angeles, accepted the position of rabbi at Bnai Jeshurun., with the mission of reviving the congregation.

Attuned to the character and needs of the community, Rabbi Meyer guided B'nai Jeshurun to become a thriving liberal synagogue that attracted thousands of Jewish people. In the nine short years from 1984 to 1993, this dying synagogue became a magnet for Jews within and outside the neighborhood. The unique and spiritually uplifting religious services and challenging theology espoused by Rabbi Meyer, an agenda that emphasized social action as a central part of the synagogue's principles, ecumenical work with Christian and Muslim clergy and a leading role in the peace movement in regard to the Arab-Israeli conflict, led to the rapid growth of the congregation, which became a model for many other synagogues in the United States.

Not long after his arrival, Rabbi Meyer recruited his former students in Argentina, Rabbi J. Rolando Matalon and Cantor Ari Priven, to come to Bnai Jeshurun. The synagogue also discontinued its affiliation with the United Synagogue of Conservative Judaism.

Rabbi Meyer died of cancer in 1993 at age 63. At his death, Bnai Jeshurun had a membership of more than 1,100 families.

Today, Bnai Jeshurun operates on a $5 million annual budget, including upkeep of its facility and rent at a nearby church to handle the overflow on Saturday mornings. They have separate congregational offices at 2109 Broadway, and have just repurchased the Hebrew School[132] building which they had sold out of desperation thirty years earlier. They maintain a lunch program and homeless shelter; a program to visit the sick and comfort mourners; and myriad study and social action programs.

It is difficult to find an empty seat at a Friday night or Shabbat morning service, and lines usually form before the doors open.

The history of Bnai Jeshurun is an instructive tale. Unfortunately, rabbinical success stories are few and far between. The more typical experience is at best mediocrity and at worst incompetence. Had Rabbi Meyer not come along at the last minute, or, had Bnai Jeshurun hired an "available" rabbi it would not exist today. Rabbi Meyer was a charismatic man who brought vision and innovation to a very tired synagogue. The changes that he espoused: an orchestra playing during the service, the cantor sitting on the side in front of a keyboard singing into a microphone, congregants dancing in the aisles, rhythmic clapping, and an overwhelming feeling of mysticism and spirituality, were not acceptable to the United Synagogue of Conservative Judaism.

Today, rabbinical schools are turning out scholars — not innovators and these well educated, sincere, mild mannered, gentle souls who have excelled at religious scholarship, and know little else, are perhaps more damaging to their synagogues and to Judaism as a whole than even the ravages of time.

---

132 There are approximately 320 students in the Bnai Jeshurun Hebrew School.

It [Is] the Best of Times, It [Is] the Worst of Times

The Pew Forum on Religion & Public Life, A Project of the Pew Research Center reports that there are about six million Jews in the Unites States. Of these, approximately 30% are married to a non-Jew; 86% of American Jews earn over $50,000, and 46% earn over $100,000. In fact, a greater percentage of Jews earn over $100,000 than any other religious group.

Of the six million American Jews, 46%[133], or roughly two and three quarter million, attend Synagogues at least once a year. Surprisingly, only nine percent of those Jews who attend synagogue are Orthodox. A much greater percentage by far, (31%) describe themselves as "Just Jewish".

And, nearly 60% of the adult Synagogue attendees are younger than fifty-five.

This represents a tremendous opportunity for the Jewish community. The potential market is young, affluent, and not ideologically committed. Most commercial marketers would be thrilled if they had such an opportunity.

So, in many ways, this is the best of times. This is a time when a creative synagogue can make a tremendous impact. There is a large potential market, the audience is accessible, the product is already proven, but the delivery channels need to be reexamined. This reexamination is a disruptive, onerous and painful, yet necessary process. Change is always difficult to accept, and, as we have seen, in the religious world it is often perceived as an insurmountable obstacle. But on occasion, as we have seen in the preceding chapters, when the need is great enough and the circumstances permit, the Jewish world has been willing change.

James Gleick writing in the *New York Times* about change ("Books and Other Fetish Objects", July 17, 2011), says that in June of 2011, the British Library announced a project with Google to digitize 40 million pages of books, pamphlets and periodicals dating to the French Revolution. This disturbed many highly respected bibliophiles who objected to this major change in the way ancient books are perceived. They saw this effort as

---

133   The statistics cited in this chapter are from the Pew Research Center and the 2000-2001 National Jewish Population Survey sponsored by the United Jewish Communities and the Jewish federation system.

diluting the essence of the rare book experience. But, as Gleick points out, a historic manuscript is merely an object "a talisman — [like] the coffin at a funeral. It deserves to be honored, but the soul has moved on."

The lesson that must be learned by the Jewish community is that the old synagogue experience, as precious as it once was, is merely an experience; a talisman that deserves to be honored. And now it is time to move on.

The synagogue experience that traditional Jews so covet and venerate was, as we have seen, a product of the religious awakening that occurred in the eighteenth and nineteenth century. It responded well to the needs of the newly reborn Jewish world, and it was adapted to the needs of the immigrants to America at the start of the twentieth century. It was valid and relevant and vibrant then. Now it needs to be modified. History has a way of fooling us. We think that because something exists, it has always existed. But that is simply not true. Things are constantly evolving and the twentieth century synagogue is not at all like the nineteenth century synagogue; and the nineteenth century synagogue was not at all like the eighteenth century synagogue. Very simply, the synagogue, and the rabbinate as we know it must be changed if Judaism is to survive.

"Easier said than done," is the usual reaction — and it is correct. Old policies die hard but unless they are replaced by new policies they *will* die and they will take their synagogues and institutions with them. The dustbin of modern Jewish history is filled with failed synagogues and institutions, yet the Jewish community continues to use the same old mold and to produce the same old product and the failures accelerate. Einstein's famous definition of insanity: "Doing the same thing over and over again and expecting different results," absolutely applies.

SEIZE THE MOMENT

There is an old Japanese proverb that says "Vision without action is a daydream, action without vision is a nightmare." Rabbinical students can *dream* of leading a congregation — of inspiring them with both words and deeds — of overwhelming them with knowledge and perception. But without a clear plan of action *and* the skills and knowledge to implement that plan, both the student and his congregation are doomed to failure.

In order to take advantage of the window of opportunity that was described in the last chapter, rabbinical schools must begin teaching business development skills. Rabbis should know how to write a mission statement, how to articulate a vision, and how to make them happen. These skills are as important for the success or failure of a rabbi and a congregation as any Talmudic exegesis.

Synagogues are large institutions. In any other environment they would be considered "big business." For example, according to the National Jewish Population Survey[134], the *average* number of members of a Reform synagogue is nine hundred and thirty nine. Although synagogue budgets can run into the millions of dollars, most synagogues are managed like "mom and pop" businesses, whereas they should be managed like the big businesses that they are. Rabbinical students should be taught to analyze marketing opportunities, develop marketing strategies, and manage and deliver marketing programs. They should understand and hope to achieve the management skills necessary for management of a twenty-first century organization. They should learn sales techniques and the importance of personal appearance. They should be graded on their social skills, on their coaching ability and on their public relations proficiency.

The days of the all-powerful, all-knowing rabbi are over for the great majority of the Jewish people, and a new, savvy rabbi is appearing. This rabbi understands that it is his responsibility to make Judaism interesting, attractive, and responsive to the modern True Jews. This is not, as some right wing Orthodox Jews might claim, "Judaism-Lite"; it is rather the core of a new Judaism for the twenty-first century. This new savvy rabbi must use whatever tools are available to make Judaism more accessible, more interesting, more exciting, more hospitable, more stimulating, and more successful than ever in its history. As Marshall McLuhan said, "The medium is the message" meaning that there is a symbiotic relationship by which the medium (the rabbi and the synagogue and their individual and collective image) influences how the message is perceived.

---

134   See Appendix.

This is *not* the time to bemoan the fate of the Jewish people. It is rather the time to reinvent Judaism once again. In the eighteenth century Israel ben Eliezer, known as the Ba'al Shem Tov, founded Hasidic Judaism and changed the face of Judaism forever and just a few years later Moses Mendelssohn developed the Haskalah movement which opened the door for the development of all the modern Jewish denominations. Today we again have an opportunity, just like the opportunity that arose in the eighteenth century, to *Re-Form* both Judaism and its leaders into a new model.

True Jews and the Entrepreneurial Rabbi

In the beginning of this book we discussed how the Pharisees, following the destruction of the Temple and the beginning of the Jewish Diaspora created a rabbinic centered religion. As leaders of a people that had lost its foundation, they reformulated Judaism based on a new model. Essentially, they recognized that the Jews, having lost their core, needed a new strong central authority and a new set of rules to live by. Within a few hundred years they developed the Talmud and Halachah, and these two monumental achievements remained the heart of the new Judaism for the next two thousand years.

We have also seen that in the fifteen hundred years following the firm establishment of rabbinic Judaism an increasingly large percentage of Jews chose to live outside of the rabbinic sphere and that, in the eighteenth and nineteenth centuries, as a result of changes both within Judaism and within society as a whole, millions of these unaffiliated Jews began to reaffiliate with Judaism.

But in the late twentieth century this trend to reaffiliate lost steam and began to slide back toward the conditions that had existed prior to the eighteenth century: Disaffection with the liberal Jewish communities became more and more apparent as the strength and influence of the Orthodox community increased.

In response to this trend, the liberal Jewish communities used a kind of shotgun approach: firing in as many different directions as possible, hoping to hit something. Some became more liberal, some more traditional, some added various features, and some just sat tight and hoped for the best. Through it all they doggedly retained their institutions and in spite of a deteriorating environment, their governing bodies attempted to remain faithful to their historic ideals. But, though the structure of the institutions remained the same, their effectiveness declined.

They held their meetings and discussed their financial difficulties, and their loss of membership, and the general disaffection of the community. In some cases they decided to downsize, and in some cases they decided to seek a more dynamic and attractive rabbi, or cantor, or educator. In some cases they decided to move or merge, in some cases they decided to take in community groups to help cover the costs, and in some unfortunate cases they decided to close their synagogue and move on.

All of these fateful decisions were made by a volunteer, unpaid, unprofessional and often inexperienced lay board of directors consisting of members of the congregation. These generous and devoted people gave up nights that they might have spent with family and friends in order to manage the affairs of the synagogue. But sadly, for the most part, although well intentioned, the members of these synagogue boards were ill equipped to manage a synagogue.

What they needed is a professional — someone who knows how to run a synagogue — someone whose *only* job is running the synagogue, someone who has been trained in synagogue management. There are people like that, and some of the larger synagogues have them — they're usually called executive directors. But in the end, they answer to and are controlled by the (lay) board of directors whose members change every one or two years. They also answer to and are controlled by the rabbi who is the final arbiter on things both religious and communal. In some cases they are also subject to the demands of the cantor and the Hebrew School principal each of whom often have their own bailiwick and their own advocates on the board. Politics, as we all know, plays an all too important role in the management and the character of a synagogue. Plus, each of the most active families usually also has its own special agenda.

For example, if one family or group of families is more vocal or persuasive in their demands the board generally accedes to their requirements.

If one family contributes a substantial amount of money or time to the synagogue, the board generally follows their demands. If one family participates in services more frequently than the others, the board generally follows their demands. Upon occasion the demands of these influential families may conflict with each other and this conflict might eventually give birth to another synagogue.[135]

Sometimes an "executive director" is hired to moderate and ameliorate these conflicts and to put the synagogue on a successful track. But usually, although the background of the "executive director" might include religious training, or experience as a Hebrew School teacher or principal, or perhaps experience within another segment of the Jewish community they are rarely equipped to deal with management, marketing, and social issues. They may be familiar with building management or accounting or fund raising, but only the exceptional director has had the necessary social and interpersonal training necessary for capable synagogue management. Plus they are rarely MBA's and do not have the necessary marketing and management skills to move the synagogue forward.

Prior to the development of the Reform movement in the nineteenth century most synagogues were managed as a monopoly by the rabbi. In the shtetle and in the ghettos, the rabbi was the sole head of the Jewish community and was the final arbiter of everything. The synagogue building belonged to the rabbi (in fact his family usually lived upstairs or next door). All of the prayer books and torahs, and books in the library belonged to the rabbi. And when the rabbi died it all passed on to his designated heir, who was often his eldest son[136]. Those who objected to this set-up were free to leave.

But then, when Reform Judaism took hold, the model changed. The management of synagogues became more egalitarian, and the "commu-

---

135 There is an old Jewish joke about a Jew who is rescued after many years of living alone on an island. On the island are two synagogues. When asked why one person would need two synagogues the man explains, "That's the synagogue I go to, and that's the one I wouldn't set foot in!"

136 The Succession feud in the Satmar community is a good example. In 1999, Rabbi Moshe, the head of the Satmar, designated his third son Rabbi Zalman as his successor. This infuriated the allies of his eldest son, Rabbi Aaron, and the movement divided into two hostile camps — one located in Williamsburg, Brooklyn, and the other in Orange County, NY.

nity" owned the synagogue. The synagogue, which had previously been supported by funds donated personally to the rabbi and by payments for services performed by the rabbi; now was a communal entity that was owned and managed by the community, and the rabbi, was theoretically, an employee[137] of the synagogue. The new communal synagogue was supported by a combination of voluntary contributions, fees for High Holiday seats, and membership dues. The theory was: "If you live in the community, even if you only attend the synagogue a few times a year — or even never — you still have an obligation to support the synagogue."

This formula was effective though most of the twentieth-century. Healthy competition grew as new synagogues in different denominations arose and community members had choices of more than one synagogue. Soon worshipers could choose from Reform, Conservative, Reconstructionist, Modern Orthodox, Secular Humanist, Egalitarian, Mechitzah, ultra Orthodox,[138] and dozens of other liturgical variations.

The one thing that all of the synagogues in any of the various competing denominations had in common is that they were all run by a lay board of directors; and with very few exceptions, they are all struggling.

THE ENTREPRENEURIAL RABBI AND THE SELF SUSTAINING SYNAGOGUE

In the first five hundred years of the Jewish Diaspora, millions of True Jews left the fold and went off on their own to fend for themselves. For the next thousand years these adventurous and entrepreneurial Jews forged their own path. But then, in the late eighteenth century, when Judaism finally began opening its doors to them, they returned in fantastic numbers. Today, True Jews are once again leaving the fold in increasing numbers and Judaism must find a new way to reopen its doors.

That new way is through the introduction and development of The Entrepreneurial Rabbi and the Self Sustaining Synagogue.

---

137 In a great many cases the rabbi was given a "lifetime" contract so his employment and his future would be secure.

138 In some of the more cult-like Hassidic groups like the Satmar, the rabbi still owns the synagogue.

The *entrepreneurial rabbi* is a highly trained individual. He possesses both a legitimate "smicha"[139] and an advanced degree in synagogue management and marketing. He has all of the rabbinic training necessary to qualify as a certified rabbi in his denomination plus he has highly developed management and marketing skills and the public presence of a political candidate. He is well equipped to initiate and manage the self sustaining synagogue.

The *self sustaining synagogue* is initiated and managed exclusively by the rabbi. Its purpose is to provide all necessary services to the Jewish community on an as-needed, fee-for-services basis. It is entrepreneurial in the sense that it does not depend on the largess of the community, but instead, like every other service business, it derives its income from the services it performs. It is wholly owned and operated by the entrepreneurial rabbi and his employees.

Like every good marketer, the entrepreneurial rabbi searches for a community that offers an opportunity for him to open a self sustaining synagogue. He derives his income from the worshipers and affiliates of his synagogue and also from the services that he and his staff perform. He does whatever is necessary to attract and establish a congregation. In some cases he might be a great scholar and people might want to be near him to be taught by him. In some cases he might be a brilliant musician and people might want to attend his joyous musical services. In some cases he might be a nice, warm, individual who provides a welcoming atmosphere. In some cases he might be a brilliant speaker, or a very good cook, or great with children, or an all around good friend, or a good listener, or a brilliant coach, or a family therapist, or maybe all of the above.

What differentiates this entrepreneurial rabbi and his self sustaining synagogue from the old model is that both the synagogue and the rabbi *sell* what they do. If people want to be members (think of subscribers to netflix) of this synagogue they pay a membership fee and they receive a basic package of privileges. There might be differing categories of membership such as "all inclusive" or a fee for specific services. For example, if they want to take a class they pay for the class. If they have children who need to be educated they pay for that education. If they are get-

---

139 Literally this is the "laying on of hands" but it means "ordination".

ting married or have marital problems, if they have a birth or a bris or a baby-naming or a funeral, they pay for the services rendered. What they don't pay for is "obligation." There *is* no obligation in the self sustaining synagogue with an entrepreneurial rabbi and there is no (Jewish) guilt.

And every day, the rabbi, like every other merchant, must sell himself and his synagogue. He must convince enough people to attend synagogue and use his services so that he can make a living. He must constantly seek ways to improve his services so that he not only retains his current members but also attracts a larger clientele.

He might have a specific building in which all of the services will be performed or he might rent office space or a storefront. He might go out into the community and perform his services in people's houses, or he might perform the services in his own house. He might buy or borrow or rent prayer books and torahs and talises from whatever sources are available. It is up to the entrepreneurial rabbi to build his congregation and he will use whatever skills he learned as a marketer to make his synagogue as attractive as possible.

The concept of the entrepreneurial rabbi is very much the same as the entrepreneurial accountant or lawyer or doctor. If he's good at it he will make a good living. If not, then he should choose another line of work.

Of necessity, the structure and fabric of the new self sustaining synagogue will be as different from the present traditional model as the new Jewish "temples" of the nineteenth century were from the old rabbinic community model. It will evolve, in the same way that synagogues have evolved since the introduction of the nineteenth century model. It will probably no longer be tied to a particular religious denomination, but will pick and choose aspects from the various denominations that will be meaningful to its specific congregation. It might, for example, be more traditional in its ritual but less traditional in its observances. It might espouse specific aspects of disparate movements blurring the distinctions between the various divisions of Jewish theology.

Like the True Jew at the beginning of the Diaspora, and the True Jew at the dawn of the Jewish renaissance of the eighteenth and nineteenth centuries, the True Jew of the Twenty-First century is tough and demanding. He isn't concerned with obligations, he wants service. He might want his children to be educated by talented and inspiring teachers, he might want to celebrate Shabbat and the holidays in a way that is meaningful to him. He might want to be part of a Jewish community that is sensitive and responsive to his needs. He is ambitious and successful and he wants his success to be rewarded in a way that is meaningful to him. He chooses his neighborhood, his home, his gardener, his doctor, his children's schools, his financial advisor, his interior decorator, and all the other accoutrements of success based on an evaluation of their quality, relevance, and affordability. He should be able to choose his rabbi and his synagogue based on the same criteria. He wants the best that he can afford for himself and his family, and he is not willing to settle for just what is available.

Every person has their own criteria for "best." This tension between the True Jew's desires and the entrepreneurial rabbi's offering is known as the Value Proposition. The rabbi has to convince his customers that his offering or product or service will add more "value" to their lives than that of his competitors.

The entrepreneurial rabbi will choose to locate his self sustaining synagogue in a community where he perceives an opportunity — not just an altruistic opportunity to fill a need, but a selfish opportunity to earn a living. He will advertise his services in the local newspaper, go where the people are, like street fairs and shopping centers, and use all the marketing techniques that he has learned to attract and grow a congregation. He will offer whatever services are needed, wherever and whenever they are needed. And he will learn to adapt his offering to the needs of the community – not the other way around.

His congregation might meet in a synagogue, or in a store front, or in someone's home, or anywhere that is convenient. Interestingly, there is no word in the Hebrew language for synagogue, the closest is Bais Kneses which literally means the house of entry. The word synagogue dates from the twelfth century and means assembly. It is probably of French or Greek origin. The self sustaining synagogue community might consist of and cater to intermarried families, or religious families, or intellectually curious families, or spiritual families or gay families; and each of the entrepreneurial rabbis will understand and be responsive to the needs of his unique population.

Although the community run synagogue and the "employee" rabbi were once considered traditional, they are not original elements of Biblical or Diaspora Judaism., and their replacement is a natural evolutionary process.

We True Jews have fought, suffered, and refined our beliefs for over two thousand years. And over that time our needs and wants have evolved; and so has our religion. In the same way that the world of communication was unable, a scant fifty years ago, to anticipate the advent and effect of the computer; it seems impossible today, to visualize the new Judaism. But all the pieces are in place for astounding growth and success, and the time for the birth of that new Judaism is now. How fortunate our granddaughter Isabel is to be a True Jew at this time in history; to be present at the rebirth and reconfiguration of Judaism; to be able to find new meaning and relevance in her Judaism; and to join her True Jewish friends in the twenty-first century whose parents may be committed or disaffected or intermarried or whatever but are all eager participants in the evolution of the new Judaism.

APPENDICES

APPENDIX A: THE CASE OF THE MISSING JEWS

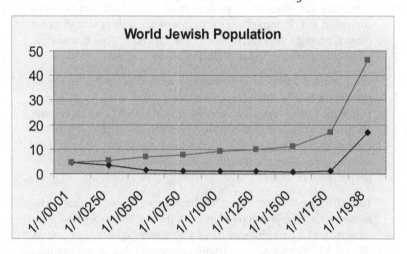

World Jewish Population

The above chart shows the world Jewish population over nearly two millennia in the Diaspora. The lower line (with diamonds) shows the actual population. The upper line (with the squares) shows the potential Jewish population if it had kept pace with the world's growth rate. For the first five hundred years of the Common Era the world population grew from 200 million to 300 million; an increase of 50%. The Jewish population, during the same period declined 69%, from 4.5 million to 1.4 million. Had the Jewish population kept pace with the world population, it would have been 6.75 million. For the next thousand years, as the world population increased 375%, the Jewish population actually declined.

APPENDIX B: NATIONAL JEWISH POPULATION SURVEY 2000–2001

To compare the historic estimates with current statistical data, the following is excerpted from the National Jewish Population Survey which was conducted in 2000–2001:

> American Jews possess many strengths, face important challenges, and exhibit notable diversity. They maintain frequent points of involvement in Jewish religious and ethnic group life, but many are disengaged from the Jewish community. As a group, American Jews have relatively high educational levels and socio-economic status, but significant pockets of poverty and social service needs also exist within the population. Intermarriage, delayed marriage and low fertility rates constitute challenges to Jewish continuity. The diversity across these areas — religious, cultural, social, communal and demographic — is truly striking, making simple, global characterizations difficult to reach. The American Jewish landscape, while full of common themes, is also marked by systematic variation.

> This portrait of American Jews emerges from the National Jewish Population Survey (NJPS) 2000-01, a representative survey of the Jewish population in the United States sponsored by United Jewish Communities and the Jewish federation system. This report presents findings on several demographic topics; Jewish connections and engagement; intermarriage; and three special topics, the elderly, immigrants and those living below the poverty line.

> The NJPS questionnaire was administered to 4,523 respondents who represent the total Jewish population. Of these, 4,220 respondents with stronger Jewish connections received a "long-form" questionnaire. An additional 303 respondents with Jewish connections that are not as strong answered a "short-form" questionnaire. The short-form version consisted of a subset of questions on the long form, omitting many questions on specifically Jewish topics. As a result, some data — for example, many demographic items — are available for the entire population. Other data, especially on many Jewish subjects, are restricted to a more engaged population of Jews represented by respondents to the long form.

Jewish Connections

> At the heart of NJPS are findings related to Jewish connections, including Jewish identity, participation in Jewish religious, cultural and ethnic life, affiliation with communal organizations, Jewish education and ties to Israel. A selection of approximately two dozen indicators of Jewish con-

nections demonstrates the patterns of strengths, challenges and diversity that characterize the American Jewish population.

Most American Jewish adults observe in some way the High Holidays, Passover and Chanukah. Majorities also read a Jewish newspaper or magazine or books with Jewish content, regard being Jewish as very important, and report that half or more of their close friends are Jewish. Taken together, these findings point to widespread engagement in Jewish family life around certain holidays, cultural involvement, an inner commitment to being Jewish, and significant Jewish friendship ties.

In contrast, smaller proportions — generally between a quarter and a third — report involvement in other religious and communal activities. Among these are always or usually lighting Shabbat candles, keeping kosher at home, attending religious services monthly or more, belonging to a JCC or other Jewish organization, making a personal or household contribution to Jewish federation campaigns, volunteering under Jewish auspices, participating in adult Jewish education programs, and having visited Israel two or more times.

Between these two extremes are a moderate proportion of American Jews, from about a third to nearly a half, who engage in a variety of Jewish behaviors. Most prominent among these are belonging to a synagogue either personally or as a household (46%). Among those who belong to a synagogue, they divide as follows: 39% Reform, 33% Conservative, 21% Orthodox, 3% Reconstructionist, and 4% other types.

In addition, moderate proportions of Jews have visited Israel at least once, make a personal or household donation to a Jewish cause outside the federation system, use the Internet for Jewish purposes, and participate in a variety of cultural activities such as watching a movie or listening to a tape, CD or record with Jewish content. In short, the diversity of possibilities for Jewish engagement is as great as the diversity of levels of engagement. Selective types of connections consistently appeal to large proportions of Jews, while other forms of engagement remain the province of those who are more religious, communally involved and culturally active.

Communal Affiliation And Jewish Connections

Traditionally, formal institutions have been vital to the Jewish community. The centrality of synagogues, JCCs and other Jewish organizations is so profound that Jewish leadership frequently distinguishes between "affiliated" and "unaffiliated" members of the Jewish population.

Institutional affiliation is not a constant over the life course. Marriage and parenthood, economic status, friends, residential location, Jewish commitment and other factors combine to influence who joins Jewish institutions. Though causal directions are difficult to determine, institutionally affiliated Jews more often engage in other domains of Jewish life than Jews who are not organizational members.

To examine affiliation-related differences in Jewish involvement, a measure of affiliation was constructed based on synagogues, JCCs and other Jewish organizations. Those with no such memberships total 44% of adult Jews and are called "unaffiliated." The affiliated divide evenly into two groups: those with one membership (28%) are called "moderately affiliated," and those with two or more memberships (28%) are regarded as "highly affiliated."

Substantial differences in Jewish connections and engagement exist between the unaffiliated and the moderately and highly affiliated. The unaffiliated differ most dramatically from the two affiliated groups with respect to religious service attendance, adult Jewish education, charitable giving to Jewish causes, volunteering under Jewish auspices, and selected observances like lighting Shabbat candles and keeping kosher at home. Differences between the unaffiliated and the affiliated are smaller but still significant regarding friendships with other Jews, connections to Israel, the use of media with Jewish content, subjective importance of being Jewish, and observances such as fasting on Yom Kippur, lighting Chanukah candles and holding or attending a Passover Seder.

In every case, the highly affiliated are even more engaged in other aspects of Jewish life than the moderately affiliated, but the differences between these groups are not substantial in most cases. The major divide in the population is between those with at least one institutional affiliation and those with none.

Jewish Connections	All Jews 100%	Unaffiliated 44%	Moderately Affiliated 28%	Highly Affiliated 28%
Half or more of close friends are Jewish	52	41	68	81
Hold/attend Passover Seder	77	58	88	96
Light Chanukah candles	72	69	90	94
Fast on Yom Kippur	59	39	69	80
Light Shabbat candles	28	8	36	50
Keep kosher at home	21	8	25	36
Attend Jewish religious service monthly or more	27	5	34	56
Belong to synagogue	46			
Belong to JCC	21			
Belong to other Jewish organization	28			

Jewish Connections	All Jews 100%	Unaffiliated 44%	Moderately Affiliated 28%	Highly Affiliated 28%
Volunteer under Jewish auspices	25	6	27	52
Participate in adult Jewish education	24	6	29	47
Visited Israel	35	25	44	58
Visited Israel two or more times	20	9	21	35
Feel emotionally attached to Israel		48	74	85
Contribute to federation campaign	30	12	31	57
Contribute to Jewish cause (not federation)	41	18	58	80
Read Jewish newspaper/magazine	65			
Read books with Jewish content	55			
Listen to tape, CD, record with Jewish content	45			
Watch movie with Jewish content	44			
Use Internet for Jewish purposes	39			
Regard being Jewish as very important	52	33	59	74

There is a remarkable similarity between the NJPS percentages and the estimates that we have been using regarding the Jewish population from 500 CE to 1750. In the case of our estimates for the historic Jewish population, 16% of the Jews might be considered highly affiliated. In the case of the NJPS, 28% of today's Jewish population is rated as "highly affiliated," but of these only 56% attend Jewish religious services monthly or more. That level of affiliation would not have been acceptable in the closely knit rabbinic communities. So, comparing apples to apples, the actual percentage of NJPS Jews who might be considered *highly* affiliated according to rabbinic standards, is closer to 16% — the same as our historic estimates.

APPENDIX C: JEWISH POPULATION: PATRIARCHS TO THE PRESENT

The chart on page 173, taken from *A Historical Atlas of the Jewish People: From the Time of the Patriarchs to the Present* by Eli Barnavi (Schocken Books, 1994) graphically illustrates historic Jewish population growth. In the year 1 CE, the world's total population was 250 million. In that same year the world's Jewish population was moderately estimated at 4.5 million. By 1750 the world's total population had increased three and a half times to 700 million. If the Jewish population had kept pace with the general population it would have been over 10 million. But instead of growing, the Jewish population declined to 1 million.

Theodore Mommsen, who was generally regarded as the greatest classicist of the 19th century estimated that at the beginning of the first century, there were about 4.5 million Jews spread all over the Roman and the Persian empires. There were three large centers: Israel, Egypt, and Babylon.

But by the sixth century, according to Mommsen, the world Jewish population had shrunk to approximately one million, with about 80 percent living in Mesopotamia, which is modern day Iraq. Only 10 percent of the original Jewish community remained in Israel and there were almost no Jews in Egypt and the rest of the Byzantine Empire. We now know that this latter statement is incorrect. There were large well established and flourishing Jewish communities in Algeria, Ethiopia, Libya, Morocco, Syria, Tunisia, and Yemen. Egypt always had a Jewish population.

Mommsen does not even mention the Bene Israel and the Cochin communities of India, nor the Jews of Armenia or the archeologically substantiated presence of Jews in Georgia.

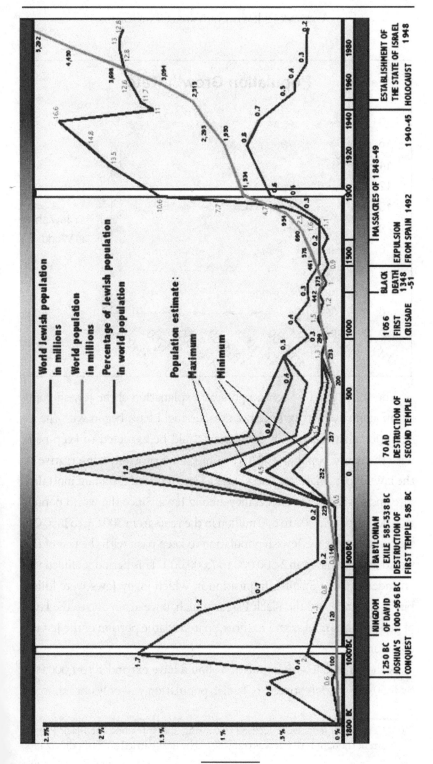

APPENDIX D: JEWISH VS. WORLD POPULATION

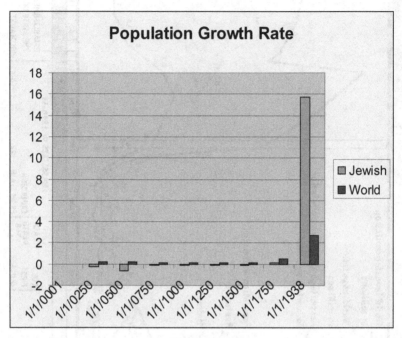

The above chart presents a possible explanation of the Jewish population anomaly that we have been discussing. I have begun with the assumption that the Jewish population could be expected to keep pace with the world population. This assumption is probably conservative as the laws of personal cleanliness and kashrus reduced the infant mortality rate and extended life expectancy among Jews. Since the world population doubled from 300 to 600 million in the years from 500 CE to 1650 CE, we could expect the Jewish population to keep pace with the rest of the world and double from 3,500,000 to 7,000,000. This period included the crusades and the Spanish Inquisition in which many Jews were killed, but it also included the Black Plague which, once again due to the laws of personal cleanliness and kashrus, spared a large portion of the Jewish community[140].

Although the Jewish population should have expanded to 7,000,000 by 1650, the *official* estimate of Jewish population was only one million. I

---

140   As a result, Jews were accused of causing and spreading the Black Plague. Current thought is that it was transmitted by fleas carried on the bodies of rats.

Year	World Population	Jewish Population Should Be	Official Jewish Census	Unaffiliated or Uncounted	Killed or Converted (In)/Out	Adjusted Population Should Be	Probable Jewish Population
500	300,000,000	3,500,000					3,500,000
1650	600,000,000	7,000,000	1,000,000	5,000,000	1,000,000	7,000,000	6,000,000
1750	750,000,000	8,750,000	1,100,000	5,900,000	500,000	7,500,000	7,000,000
1850	1,171,000,000	13,650,000	4,600,000	5,900,000	420,000	10,920,000	10,500,000
1900	1,608,000,000	18,700,500	11,000,000	—	3,385,000	14,385,000	11,000,000
1940	2,216,000,000	25,806,690	16,700,000	—	(1,520,000)	15,180,000	16,700,000

inserted the seven million figure in the "Adjusted Population Should Be" column. I then estimated, based on historic reports, that one million former Jews had either converted or been killed and that the Jewish population was really only six million. But since the official population count in

1650 shows only one million Jews, I put these "missing" five million Jews in the "Unaffiliated or Uncounted" column.

By 1750 the world population had increased another twenty-five percent. So, I increased the "Adjusted Population" by twenty-five percent as well, to 7,500,000. But official census figures from 1750 peg the Jewish population at 1,100,000. I estimated that 500,000 Jews either were killed or converted during that period, which leaves 5,900,000 Jews who were unaffiliated. Both of these numbers are logical. The "converted" figure is in agreement with historic estimates, and the unaffiliated number reflects the continuity in this category.

The numbers for 1850 continue this pattern as may be expected. The same number of Jews left the religion and the same number of Jews were unaffiliated. But then, starting around 1850, as a result of the upheavals in Judaism and in society as a whole, the number of Jews leaving Judaism skyrocketed to nearly ten times the previous periods. This too is in agreement with contemporary estimates.

By 1850 modern census methods were being used and the population numbers were reasonably accurate. All people in a country were counted and then they were subdivided into religious segments. The likelihood of Jews falling through the cracks or disappearing into the countryside was largely removed as everyone was required to declare their religion. The catchall category of "unaffiliated or uncounted" was no longer relevant, and internal Jewish counts of that period are unreliable.

The following is from the Jewish Encyclopedia under the listing: [Jewish population in] Ancient and medieval times:

> The Torah contains a number of statements as to the number of (adult, male) Jews that left Egypt, the descendants of the seventy sons and grandsons of Jacob who took up their residence in that country. Altogether, including Levites, the number given is 611,730. For non-Levites, this represents men fit for military service, i.e. between twenty and sixty years of age; among the Levites the relevant number is those obligated in temple service (males between twenty and fifty years of age). This would imply a population of about 3,000,000. The Census of David is said to have recorded 1,300,000 males over twenty years of age, which would imply a population of over 5,000,000. The number of exiles who returned from Babylon is given at 42,360. Tacitus declares that Jerusalem at its fall contained 600,000 persons; Josephus, that there were as many as 1,100,000, of

whom 97,000 were sold as slaves. It is from the latter that most European Jews are descended. These appear (writes Jacobs) to be all the figures accessible for ancient times, and their trustworthiness is a matter of dispute. 1,100,000 is comparable to the population of the largest cities that existed anywhere in the world before the 19th century, but geographically the Old City of Jerusalem is just a few per cent of the size of such cities as ancient Rome, Constantinople, Edo period Tokyo and Han Dynasty Xi'an. The difficulties of commissariat in the Sinai desert for such a number as 3,000,000 have been pointed out by John William Colenso.

In the Hadrianic war of CE 132–135, 580,000 Jews were slain, according to Cassius Dio (lxix. 14). According to Theodor Mommsen, in the first century C.E. there were no less than 1,000,000 Jews in Egypt, in a total of 8,000,000 inhabitants; of these 200,000 lived in Alexandria, whose total population was 500,000. Adolf Harnack (*Ausbreitung des Christentums*, Leipzig, 1902) reckons that there were 1,000,000 Jews in Syria at the time of Nero in the CE 60s, and 700,000 in Palestine, and he allows for an additional 1,500,000 in other places, thus estimating that there were in the first century 4,200,000 Jews in the world. Jacobs remarks that this estimate is probably excessive.

As regards the number of Jews in the Middle Ages, Benjamin of Tudela, about 1170, enumerates altogether 1,049,565; but of these 100,000 are attributed to Persia and India, 100,000 to Arabia, and 300,000 to an undecipherable "Thanaim", obviously mere guesses with regard to the Eastern Jews, with whom he did not come in contact. There were at that time probably not many more than 500,000 in the countries he visited, and probably not more than 750,000 altogether. The only real data for the Middle Ages are with regard to special Jewish communities. The *Jewish Encyclopedia* provides a table of this data.

The Middle Ages were mainly a period of expulsions. In 1290, 16,000 Jews were expelled from England; in 1306, 100,000 from France; and in 1492, about 200,000 from Spain. Smaller but more frequent expulsions occurred in Germany, so that at the commencement of the 16th century only four great Jewish communities remained: Frankfurt, 2,000; Worms, 1,400; Prague, 10,000; and Vienna, 3,000 (Heinrich Grätz, *Geschichte der Juden* x. 29). It has been estimated that during the five centuries from 1000 to 1500, 380,000 Jews were killed during the persecutions, reducing the total number in the world to about 1,000,000. In the 16th and 17th centuries the main centers of Jewish population were in Poland and the Mediterranean countries, Spain excepted.

According to the estimate of Basnage, at the beginning of the eighteenth century the total number of European Jews was 1,360,000, and the Jews of the kingdom of Poland (including Lithuania), according to a census at the first division in 1772, numbered 308,500. As these formed the larger part of the European Jews, it is doubtful whether the total number was more than 400,000 at the middle of the eighteenth century; and, counting those in the lands of Islam, the entire number in the world at that time could not have been much more than 1,000,000.[141]

APPENDIX E: TOTAL WORLD JEWISH POPULATION AND DISTRIBUTION

This Table shows a summary of the distribution of Jews throughout the world for the years 1800 to 1948 (population in thousands).

	1800	1840	1880	1900	1914	1938	1948
Europe (Incl. Russia)	1,500	3,950	6,858	8,900	9,100	9,500	3,700
Asia	-	300	370	510	500	1,000	1,300
Africa, Middle East	1,000	198	250	375	400	600	700
North & South America	-	50	250	1,200	3,500	5,500	5,800
Australia	-	2	10	15	-	-	-
WORLD TOTAL	2,500	4,500	7,738	11,000	13,500	16,600	11,500

APPENDIX F: TIMELINE OF THE DEVELOPMENT OF

THE JEWISH PEOPLE (CE)

66–70: The Great Jewish Revolt against Roman occupation ends with destruction of the Second Temple and the fall of Jerusalem. The Sanhedrin is relocated to Yavne by Yochanan ben Zakai.

---

141 *Jewish Encyclopedia.*

100: World Population 200,000,000; World Jewish Population 4,500,000

70–200: Period of the *Tannaim:* rabbis who organized the Jewish oral law. The decisions of the *Tannaim* are contained in the Mishnah and various Midrash compilations.

73: The fall of Masada.

115–117: Second Jewish-Roman War leads to mutual killing of hundreds of thousands Jews, Greeks and Romans, ending with a total defeat of Jewish rebels.

131–135: Bar Kokhba leads a large doomed Jewish revolt against Rome. 580,000 Jews, both combatant and civilian are killed. In the aftermath of the revolt Hadrian renamed the province of Judea as Syria Palaestina, forbidding Jews to set foot in Jerusalem, except for the anniversary of the Temple's destruction, Tisha B'av.

200: The Mishnah, the standardization of the Jewish oral law as it stands today, is edited by Judah haNasi in Israel.

220–500: Period in which the sages, both Palestinian and Babylonian, discussed the Mishnah. The discussions of these scholars, who comprised eight generations in Babylonia and five in Israel, occupy most of both the *Yerushalmi* and *Bavli* Talmuds.

315–337: Conversion of Christians to Judaism is outlawed.

351–352: Another Jewish revolt is put down.

450: Redaction of Talmud Yerushalmi.

550: The main redaction of Talmud Bavli.

700–1250: Period of the Gaonim. Most Jews lived in the Muslim Arab realm (Southern Spain, North Africa, Palestine, Iraq and Yemen). Jewish communal and cultural life flowered in this period.

711: Muslim armies invade and occupy most of Spain (At this time Jews made up about 8% of Spain's population). This is the beginning of the Golden age of Jewish culture in Spain.

760: The Karaites who maintain that all of the commandments handed down to Moses were recorded in the written Torah at Mount Sinai, without additional Oral Law or explanation split off from rabbinic Judaism..

846: In Iraq, Rav Amram Gaon compiles the first logical arrangement of the prayers for every occasion in the year, together with complete texts of the Liturgy, applicable laws and customs, and the rules governing Sabbath and festival observance.

1000: World Population 275,000,000; World Jewish Population 1,400,000

900–1090: The Golden age of Jewish culture in Spain. Jews and Christians are granted exemptions from military service, the right to their own courts of law, and a guarantee of safety of their property. Jewish poets, scholars, scientists, statesmen and philosophers flourished in and were an integral part of the extensive Arab civilization.

1095–1291: Christian Crusades begin, sparking warfare with Islam in Palestine. Crusaders temporarily capture Jerusalem in 1099. Tens of thousands of Jews are killed by European crusaders throughout Europe and in the Middle East.

1135–1204: Maimonides or the Rambam writes an influential code of law (The Mishneh Torah) as well as one of the most influential philosophical works (Guide for the Perplexed) in Jewish history.

1250–1550: Period of the *Rishonim*, the medieval rabbinic sages.

1290: Jews are expelled from England.

1306–1394: Jews are repeatedly expelled from France and readmitted, for a price.

1343: Jews persecuted in Western Europe are invited to Poland.

1478: King Ferdinand and Queen Isabella of Spain begin the Spanish Inquisition.

1488–1575: Rabbi Yosef Karo writes the *Shulkhan Arukh*, the Code of Jewish Law, the standard religious law guide for Jewish behavior.

1492: Approximately 200,000 Jews are expelled from Spain, The expelled Jews relocate to the Netherlands, Turkey, Arab lands, and Judea; some eventually go to South and Central America. However, most emigrate to Poland. Many Jews remain in Spain after publicly converting to Christianity, becoming Crypto-Jews.

1492: The Ottoman Empire issues a formal invitation to the Jews expelled from Spain and Portugal and sends out ships to safely bring Jews there.

1493: Jews expelled from Sicily; as many as 137,000 exiled.

1496: Jews expelled from Portugal and from many German cities.

1500: World Population 450,000,000; World Jewish Population 900,000

1501: Jews readmitted to Lithuania.

1516: The First Jewish ghetto in Europe is established in Venice, Italy. Many others follow.

1534: First Yiddish language book published, in Poland.

1534–1572: Isaac Luria teaches Kabbalah in Jerusalem and Safed to select disciples.

1547: First Hebrew Jewish printing house established in Lublin, Poland.

1580–1764: 70 official delegates from local Jewish communities in Poland meet regularly to discuss taxation and other issues important to the Jewish community.

1623: Separate Jewish governing body *(Va'CE)* in Grand Duchy of Lithuania.

1626–1676: Rise and decline of the false Messiah Sabbatai Zevi.

1648: Jewish population of Poland reaches 450,000, Bohemia 40,000 and Moravia 25,000. Worldwide population of Jewry is estimated at 750,000.

1648–1655: The Ukrainian Cossack Bohdan Chmielnicki leads a massacre of Polish gentry and Jewry that leaves an estimated 65,000 Jews dead and a similar number of gentry.

1655: Jews readmitted to England.

1700–1760: Israel ben Eliezer, known as the Ba'al Shem Tov, founds Hasidic Judaism. He and his disciples attract many followers, and establish numerous Hasidic sects.

1729–1786: Moses Mendelssohn develops the Haskalah (Enlightenment) movement which opens the door for the development of all the modern Jewish denominations and the revival of Hebrew as a spoken language.

1750: World Population 700,000,000; World Jewish Population 1,000,000

1772–1795: Partition of Poland among Russia, Prussia and Austria.

1775: The American Revolution.

1789: The French revolution

1791: Russia creates the Pale of Settlement that includes land acquired from Poland with a huge Jewish population. The Jewish population of the Pale is 750,000; the Jewish population of Prussian and Austrian Poland is 450,000.

1800: World Population 1,000,000,000; World Jewish Population 2,500,000

1804: Napoleonic Civil Code grants religious freedom to Jews in French Empire

1820–1860: Development of Orthodox Judaism

1850: World Population 1,200,000,000; World Jewish Population 4,600,000

Mid 1800s: Beginning of classical Reform Judaism

Mid-1800s: Rabbi Israel Salanter develops the Mussar Movement advocating ethical teachings as the essence of Judaism.

Mid-1800s: Positive-Historical Judaism, later known as Conservative Judaism, is developed.

1860: Alliance Israelite Universelle, an international Jewish organization with the goal to protect Jewish rights as citizens is founded in Paris.

1860–1875: Moshe Montefiori builds Jewish neighborhoods outside of Jerusalem.

1860–1943: Henrietta Szold: educator, author, social worker and founder of Hadassah, the Women's Zionist Organization.

1861: The Zion Society is formed in Frankfurt am Main, Germany.

1862: Jews are given equal rights in Russian-controlled Poland.

1867: Jews are emancipated in Hungary.

1870–1890: Russian Zionist group set up a series of Jewish settlements in Israel, financially aided by Baron Edmond James de Rothschild; Hebrew is revived as a spoken modern language.

1870: Jews are emancipated in Italy.

1871: Jews are emancipated in Germany.

1880: World Jewish population is around 7.7 million, 90% in Europe, mostly Eastern Europe; around 3.5 million in the former Polish provinces.

1881–1884, 1903–1906, 1918–1920: Three major waves of pogroms kill tens of thousands of Jews in Russia and Ukraine. More than two million Russian Jews emigrate.

1881: The First Congress of all Zionist Unions for the colonization of Palestine is held in Romania.

1882–1903: The First Aliyah, a major wave of Jewish immigrants to build a homeland in Palestine.

1890: The term "Zionism" defined as the national movement for the return of the Jewish people to their homeland and the resumption of Jewish sovereignty in the Land of Israel is coined by Austrian Jewish publicist Nathan Birnbaum.

1897: In response to the Dreyfus affair, Theodore Herzl writes Der Judenstaat (The Jewish State), advocating the creation of a free and independent Jewish state in Israel.

1897: The Bund (General Jewish Labor Bund) is formed in Russia.

1900: World Population 1,600,000,000; World Jewish Population 11,000,000

1917: The British gain control of Palestine and issue the Balfour Declaration which gives official British support for "the establishment in Palestine of a national home for the Jewish people".

1917: The Pale of Settlement is abolished, and Jews get equal rights.

1924: There are 2,989,000 Jews in Poland (10.5% of total population). 23% of students of high schools are Jewish and 26% of students of universities[142].

1938: World Population 2,500,000,000; World Jewish Population 16,700,000

APPENDIX G: TIMELINE OF THE JEWISH COMMUNITIES OF POLAND

Late 1400s: More than 60 Jewish communities are known in Poland population is thought to be 20,000 to 30,000

1515: Rabbi Shalom Shachna founds Poland's first yeshiva in Lublin

1525–1572: Rabbi Moses Ben Israel Isserles lives in Krakow, where he founds a yeshiva and writes a commentary to the Shulchan Aruch, the Code of Jewish Law

1573: Confederation of Warsaw of 1573 guarantees religious tolerance in Poland

1500s and early 1600s: Some Jews expelled from Spain move to Poland; Jewish social, cultural and economic life flourishes; population estimated at 80,000 to 100,000

---

142 This timeline is based on information from Wikipedia. It may not have been reviewed by professional editors.

1648–49: Chmielnicki revolt and massacre brings 30 years of bloodshed and suffering to Jews in Poland; golden age in Poland ends

1700–1760: Israel ben Eliezer, known as the Ba'al Shem Tov, founds modern Chasidism

1764: Jewish population about 750,000; worldwide Jewish population estimated at 1.2 million

1772: Partitions of Poland begin between Russia, Prussia and Austria

1791: Russian government restricts Jews to the Pale of Settlement, which includes lands formerly in Poland

1800s: Tremendous growth of Jewish population (in 1781, 3,600 Jews in Warsaw or 4.5 percent of population; in 1897, 219,000 Jews in Warsaw or 33.9 percent of population)

1862: Jews are given equal rights

1897: 1.3 million Jews in Poland

Bibliography

Aishe.com. *Why the Jews, The Racial Theory.* International.aish.com

Balter, Michael, "Tracing the Roots of Jewishness." *Science Now* (June 2010)

Barnavi, Eli. *A Historical Atlas of the Jewish People: From the Time of the Patriarchs to the Present.* New York: Schocken Books, 1994

Brians, Paul. Emeritus Professor of English Washington State University: WSU.edu.

Drucker, Peter. *Management Tasks Responsibilities Practices.* New York: Harper & Row, 1973.

Eban, Abba. *My People, The Story of the Jews.* New York: Behrman House, 1968

Gladwell, Malcolm. "Getting in." *The New Yorker* (October, 2005)

Gleick, James. "Books and Other Fetish Objects." *The New York Times* (July 2011)

Graetz, Professor H. *History of the Jews.* Philadelphia: The Jewish Publication Society, 1891.

Jewish Encyclopedia, 1901–1906: Jewishencyclopedia.com.

Jewish Museum. *The Power of Conversation: Jewish Women and Their Salons.*

Johnson, George. "Scholars Debate Roots of Yiddish, Migration of Jews." The New York Times, (October 1996)

Kotler, Philip. *Marketing Management.* Upper Saddle River: Prentice-Hall, 2000.

Leibovitz, Liel. "A New Read of Jewish Life." *Tablet Magazine* (December 2010)

Lewis, Bernard. "Muslim Anti-Semitism." *The Middle East Quarterly* (June 1998)

Markus, David M. *The Encyclopedia of Arkansas History and Culture.* Fayetteville: University of Arkansas.

Mazumdar, Mohini Lal. *The Imperial Post Offices of British India. Calcutta.* Phila Publications, 1990.

Murray, Charles. "Jewish Genius," Commentary Magazine (April 2007)

Pew Forum on Religion & Public Life, A Project of the Pew Research Center.

Philips, Rev. Dr. A. Th. *Prayer Book for the Day of Atonement.* New York: Hebrew Publishing Company, 1931.

Raddock, Charles. *Portrait of a People.* New York: Judaica Press, 1967.

Sabbath and Festival Prayer Book. New York: The Rabbinical Assembly of America and The United Synagogue of America, 1946.

Schulweis, Harold M. Keruv, "Conversion And The Unchurched." Valley Beth Shalom Outreach Lecture I (February 2011)

Silverman, Jacob. "A New Read of Jewish Life." *Tablet Magazine* (March 2011).

Sugarman, Catriel. The Jewish Voice (February 2009)

The Jewish Federations of North America, *The National Jewish Population Study of 2000-2001*

The Tribe. www.cohen-levi.org

United Nations of Roma Victrix: UNRV.com,

Wade, Nicholas. "In DNA, New Clues to Jewish Roots." *The New York Times* (May 2002).

Zacharia, Janine, "Israel May Put Limits on Citizanship for Converts," *Washington Post* (July 2010)

Zelizer, Gerald L. "Conservative Rabbis, their movement, and American Judaism," *Judaism: A Quarterly Journal of Jewish Life and Thought* (June 1995)